CrossCurrents (ISSN 0011-1953; online ISSN 1939-3881) connects the wisdom of the heart with the life of the mind and the experiences of the body. The journal is operated through its parent organization, the Association for Public Religion and Intellectual Life (APRIL), an interreligious network of academics, activists, artists, and community leaders seeking to engage the many ways religion meets the public. Contributions to the journal exist at the nexus of religion, education, the arts, and social justice. The journal is published quarterly on behalf of the Association for Public Religion and Intellectual Life by the University of North Carolina Press.

The Association for Public Religion and Intellectual Life (formerly ARIL) is a global network of leaders, scholars, and social change agents who explore religious life, engage in intellectual inquiry, and lead ethical action in the world today. Their primary objective, especially through annual summer colloquia and *CrossCurrents*, is to bring together leading voices of our time to advocate for justice and to examine global spiritual and interreligious currents in both historical and contemporary perspectives.

A membership to APRIL includes access to *CrossCurrents* starting with Volume 58, 2008, though our partners at Project MUSE, monthly newsletters, early access to summer colloquium themes, a 40% on UNC Press books, and more. For more information, including membership and subscription rates, visit www.aprilonline.org.

This reissue of *CrossCurrents* was one of four issues published in 2011 as part of Volume 61. For a current masthead visit www.aprilonline.org.

© 2011 Association for Public Religion and Intellectual Life. All rights reserved.

ISBN 978-1-4696-6700-3 (Print)

CROSSCURRENTS

VOLUME 61, NO 3 ISSN 0011-1953

INTRODUCTION

286
Introduction: Religion in Asia Today
Pamela D. Winfield

ARTICLES

290
In the Wake of the Tsunami: Religious Responses to the Great East Japan Earthquake
Levi McLaughlin

298
Making a Space for Hope: Representing the Creative Reinvention of Japanese Mountain Asceticism in the Documentary Shugendō Now
Mark Patrick McGuire

328
The Contraction and Expansion of Shamanic Landscapes in Contemporary South Korea
Laurel Kendall

345
Prominent Nuns: Influential Taiwanese Voices
Jennifer Eichman

374
Hinduism Without Religion: Amma's Movement in America
Amanda J. Huffer

399
Negotiating Religious and National Identities in Contemporary Indonesian Islamic Education
Florian Pohl

415
An Interview with Arjia Rinpoche
Pamela D. Winfield

420
Notes on Contributors

On the Cover: Muroji Temple main pagoda c. 2001. Photo by Pamela D. Winfield.
Muroji's main pagoda stood in this spot in Nara Prefecture, Japan, for approximately 1,200 years until a violent typhoon destroyed its graceful rooflines in 1998. In studying the damage, Japanese architectural experts and art historians discovered a wealth of information regarding its original construction, ritual consecration, patronage networks and repair history. Its painstaking reconstruction from 1998-2000 shown here adds yet another layer to its sedimented history.
This image was chosen to serve as a symbol for this issue of *CrossCurrents*, which likewise seeks to expose the hidden truths, accretions of meaning and resilient aspirations of Asian religions today. As they weather the modern storms of globalization, social dislocation, and the natural disasters of the Pacific Rim, this issue demonstrates the ways in which Asian religions today are rebuilding themselves to remain ever-relevant cultural constructions that may re-enchant the modern world.

INTRODUCTION
Religion in Asia Today

Pamela D. Winfield

This issue of *CrossCurrents* is dedicated to the modern challenges facing Asia today and to the creative ways in which religions of the region are responding to natural, social and global stressors. It stems from a deliberate and intentional expansion in scope as *CrossCurrents'* readership expands via its electronic format to a worldwide audience. It also deliberately strives to introduce lesser known traditions, figures, and movements into the mainstream Hindu, Buddhist, and Muslim discourses of Asia. It is our sincere wish that these essays, which touch upon the environmental, hyper-urban, economic, gendered, educational, and political dimensions of religion in Asia and "transnational Asia" today, both instruct and inspire readers to shape informed and nuanced opinions that may ripple out to impact others.

East Asia

When the seed for this issue first germinated many months ago, no one could have anticipated that the 9.0 earthquake and tsunami in Sendai, Japan would present itself as perhaps *the* most pressing contemporary challenge to the country and to its religious groups today. Scholar of Japanese religions Levi McLaughlin (Wofford College, SC) outlines the events of March 11, 2011, and highlights the relief efforts, memorial ceremonies, and humanitarian motivations of the well-established and especially more recently established religious groups in Japan. In his brief and timely piece, McLaughlin underscores the religious ethos at the heart of secular Japan as it begins to rebuild.

Environmental scholar and activist Mark McGuire (John Abbott College, Montréal) also opens his essay with a religious response to the natural and nuclear devastation in Japan. Nestled deep in the UNESCO-protected Kumano mountain range, Tateishi Kōshō leads a special Shugendō rite and eco-pilgrimage to pray for lost souls and responsible government cleanup. Shugendō is Japan's age-old blend of mountain veneration, esoteric Buddhism, and asceticism that is designed to empower individual and collective well-being. Tateishi is now updating and offering these nature practices anew to the hyper-urbanized and increasingly disaffected (and often female) casualties of neo-liberal competition and global economic forces. As McGuire reflects on his own role in bringing Tateishi's movement to light as a scholar and film producer of the 2010 ethnographic documentary *Shugendō Now*, he engages with philosopher Ernest Bloch and cultural critic Henri Giroux's theories of "hope" to analyze the transformative potential of eco-pilgrimage for modern-day seekers.

The urban–rural divide and other effects of globalization are further taken up by anthropologist Laurel Kendall (American Museum of Natural History, NY). In an excerpt from her 2010 award-winning *Shamans, Nostalgias and the IMF: South Korean Popular Religion in Motion,* Kendall demonstrates how contemporary female shamans (*mansin*) have adapted to shifting religious landscapes and to new global realities during and after the IMF Crisis of 1997–1998. Even as urban sprawl has pushed these women out of the cities to rent mountainside *kuttang* shrines for *kut* diagnostic and remedial rituals, so too have improved trade relations between mainland China and South Korea since the 1990s facilitated the *mansins'* empowerment pilgrimages to Mt. Paektu from the Chinese side (the North Korean side is still impassible to southerners). The linkages between the global economy and the local religious practice have never been more clearly elucidated.

The next two essays extend the theme of women's power and agency in today's Asian and transnational Asian religious scenes. Jennifer Eichman (Moravian College, PA) features four pioneering Buddhist nuns in contemporary Taiwan who have been inspired by so-called humanistic or engaged Buddhism (*renjian fojiao* in Chinese). While the personalities and impact-strategies differ radically among Chen Yeng the traditionalist, Chao Hwei the activist, Kuan Ch'ien the academic aesthete, and Ching

Hai the New Age guru, they all have garnered international acclaim and support for their relief efforts, charitable works, public welfare institutions, structural justice initiatives, ecological activism, feminist leadership, food consciousness, and yes, even spiritual fashion-forwardness. Their savvy use of the Internet and other global media is notable as they compete for successful spiritual product placement in today's marketplace of ideas.

South/Southeast Asia/Himalayas

Amanda Huffer (University of California-Riverside) looks at the transnational female guru movement from a different, more critical perspective. She notes that South Asian guru figures such as Amma (lit. "Mother") employ the rhetoric of "spirituality" instead of "Hinduism" as they strive to appeal to diverse global audiences. This distinction, however, has led to some unintended consequences. On the one hand, it has led to an uncanny paradox. As the rhetoric of global spirituality in these contexts actually derives from the Hindu monistic philosophy of *Advaita Vedanta*, the neo-Vedantan discourse of non-denominational, non-religious, and non-Hindu spirituality concurrently becomes the very apotheosis of Hindu or Vedic wisdom. On the other hand, this shift in terminology has also unwittingly contributed to the spread of virulent Hindu Nationalism. That is, the new spiritual guru movements (separate from old, "traditional" Hinduism) are by definition universalizing and reductionistic (and therefore no longer identifiably distinctive or uniquely Hindu). As many diasporic communities strive to create a constructed Hindu national identity abroad, the ramifications of this seemingly innocuous discursive move are particularly grave given the physical and ideological displacements of today's global immigration flows.

Huffer's final observations about Hindu fundamentalism resonate with Florian Pohl's (Oxford College of Emory University, GA) essay on Islamic education in modern Indonesia. Pohl surveys the range of educational models in Indonesia today, from the private and state-run Islamic institutions of higher learning and *madrasahs* to the mostly independently organized *pesantrens*. He observes that Islamic education generally is marked by openness to general education, a conscious acceptance of Indonesia's rich cultural and religious diversity, and a rejection of the rhetoric of the Islamic state. In the last ten years, however, he has also observed the emergence of Islamic schools whose educational missions go beyond the mere transmission of Islamic knowledge and values to include broader social and political goals that favor a comprehensive Islamification of society and state. By situating contemporary education debates within the twentieth century's main ideological trends of democratization and Islamification, Pohl effectively argues that religion, politics, and public life in Indonesia are never far apart.

Finally, such discussions of religion and global politics cannot ignore the case of Tibet and China. A final interview with Arjia Rinpoche (Tibetan-Mongolian Buddhist Cultural Center, IN) is the pièce de résistance that occupies pride of place as the last word on "Religion in Asia Today." Arjia Rinpoche grew up navigating his way to the top tiers of modern Tibetan Buddhism under Chinese rule. In 1998, however, in a crisis of conscience, he fled his position as head abbott of the famed Kumbum Monastery and appointed tutor to the Politburo's hand-picked puppet Panchen Lama. At the time of his defection, he was the highest-ranking lama to leave Communist-occupied Tibet as the Dalai Lama. This brief but revealing interview serves as a complement to his compelling autobiography *Surviving the Dragon: A Tibetan Lama's Account of 40 Years Under Chinese Rule.*

In the end, these essays offer but a snapshot collage—a postcard from the first decade of the twenty-first century—that hopefully will shed light on some of the most pressing issues and inspiring responses to religious life in the region and beyond.

CROSSCURRENTS

IN THE WAKE OF THE TSUNAMI
Religious Responses to the Great East Japan Earthquake*

Levi McLaughlin

At 2:46 p.m. on March 11, 2011, the Tōhoku region of Japan was struck by what is now known officially in English as the Great East Japan Earthquake. Measuring 9.0 on the Rector scale, the catastrophic quake just off the coast of Miyagi Prefecture produced a massive tsunami that damaged or wiped out dozens of communities in eighteen prefectures along the northeast coastline of Honshū, the largest of the Japanese islands. It also triggered nuclear meltdown at the Fukushima No. 1 power plant, located approximately 240 km (150 miles) north of Tokyo. The official death toll of the Great East Japan Earthquake exceeds 15,000; more than 8,000 remain missing; hundreds of thousands were rendered homeless or displaced; and more will inevitably die in the years to come from injury and radiation sickness.

Scenes of destruction and human suffering in the wake of the quake and tsunami elicited worldwide support, both material and spiritual. But amid global calls for prayer and other religious responses, the most widely publicized religious response to the nation's worst disaster since the Second World War came from within Japan itself—a series of comments made by 78-year-old Tokyo Governor, Shintarō Ishihara.

Ishihara, a prize-winning novelist, stage and screen actor, and a populist hero of the Japanese right, has gained notoriety for his willingness to court controversy, but his take on the tragedy in northeastern Japan

---

*The original version of this article appeared on March 17, 2011 in the journal *Religion Dispatches*, and the following is reprinted with permission from *Religion Dispatches*. Read more at http://www.religiondispatches.org.

inspired more than the level of shock and outrage his comments ordinarily produce. On March 14, just three days into the crisis, Ishihara told reporters that he saw the tsunami as "divine punishment," or *tenbatsu*, a term usually employed in Japanese to describe a righteous and inevitable punishment of the wicked. For Ishihara, the tsunami produced by Japan's largest-ever recorded earthquake was a means of washing away the "egoism" (*gayoku* in Japanese) afflicting the Japanese people.

While the Tokyo Governor said that he felt sorry for the victims, he concluded that "We need a tsunami to wipe out egoism, which has rusted onto the mentality of Japanese over a long period of time." Ishihara, who was beginning a bid for a fourth term as Tokyo Governor at the time, was compelled to apologize publicly the next day, following comments by Miyagi Prefecture Governor Yoshihiro Murai, leader of the prefecture closest to the quake epicenter.[1] Murai condemned Ishihara and urged sympathy for the hundreds of thousands of victims suffering in northern Japan. Despite Ishihara's expression of regret, his "divine punishment" comment lingers as the most widely known religious sentiment expressed by a high-profile Japanese public figure in reaction to the current crisis. It resonates with similar remarks made in the United States following disasters, such as those by Pat Robertson in 2005, who described Hurricane Katrina as divine retribution for Supreme Court Chief Justice John Roberts upholding *Roe vs. Wade*, or the televised conversation between Robertson and Jerry Falwell on September 13, 2001, in which they characterized the attack on the Twin Towers as God's punishment for American tolerance of "abortionists," gays, feminists, and the ACLU.[2]

It is worth noting that Ishihara made his pronouncement while employees of the Tokyo power utility TEPCO and soldiers from Japan's Self-Defense Forces willingly risked death battling to contain the worst nuclear disaster since Chernobyl at the damaged Fukushima reactors. He made his comments as hundreds of thousands of victims who lost their homes and loved ones lined up patiently in freezing refugee camps to receive meager supplies of food and water. In the days following the earthquake and in the weeks of rolling power outages that followed, there were no reported cases of looting anywhere in the country, even as thousands of Tokyo blocks were left darkened and bereft of security. When the hungry refugees received food, they shared it with their neighbors. Cold, injured, bereaved, suffering from the onset of post-traumatic stress disorder, and facing the bleakest imaginable future, victims in northeastern Japan seemed only to embody the spirit of *gaman*, or "sticktoitiveness" that exemplifies the Japanese character.

Ishihara's comments struck many as an ideological rant, and one that seemed destined to haunt him in the election. Nonetheless, on April 10, 2011, Tokyoites handed Governor Ishihara a fourth consecutive victory; he won the election by a margin of nearly one million votes.[3] At least some of these voters must have agreed with Ishihara's unguarded sentiments regarding the quake and tsunami—that the Japanese people, in some sense, deserved the disaster that befell them.

Here's what mass religious mobilization looks like

Ironically, Japanese religious organizations themselves did not use the catastrophe as a chance to condemn Japanese moral failings with grim satisfaction in the manner expressed by Ishihara. While it appears as if Japan, like America, has its share of vocal public figures eager to equate disaster with apocalypse and to use mass human suffering as an excuse to propagandize, Japanese religious groups joined together—largely under the media radar—to help in the relief effort.

Even as Ishihara ranted about "divine punishment" Japanese religious organizations carried out the largest mobilization of clerics and lay adherents since the Second World War, all in the interest of aid and support. A few days after the quake, my colleague Keishin Inaba, Associate Professor of the Sociology of Religion at Osaka University, started a Japanese-language Facebook group called Faith-Based Network for Earthquake Relief in Japan, a clearing-house of newspaper articles, blog posts, tweets, and other information on relief initiatives by all sorts of religious groups operating in Japan.[4]

Here are a few examples of mass religious mobilization in the face of Japan's most tragic event in generations:

Temples, shrines, and other religious facilities across the Tōhoku region, and elsewhere, transformed into refugee centers. An article from March 16 on Asahi.com reported that the priest at the Rinzai Zen temple Jionji in Rikuzentakata village housed sixty-nine refugees who were treated by doctors and nurses from the Japan Red Cross. Seventy to eighty percent of the town's 8,000 households were wiped out by the tsunami.[5]

The head temple of Jōdo Shinshū, Japan's largest traditional Buddhist sect, canceled plans for the 750th memorial of sect founder Shinran (1173-1263) to be held at its Kyoto headquarters' temple complex Higashi Honganji. Instead, the Shinshū priesthood transformed Higashi Honganji into a dispatch center for relief supplies. Temple staff members loaded water, food, and portable stoves into trucks to be sent to the afflicted region, and they turned their famous garden Shōseien into a center for fundraising; and this was at a time when the 115 Higashi Honganji Jōdo Shinshū temples in Iwate, Miyagi, and Fukushima Prefectures were damaged, clergy in Sendai were known to have been killed, and the sect was unable to make contact with seven temples.

Meanwhile, leaders of the Pure Land Buddhist sect Jōdoshū reported that they were unable to contact approximately twenty of the 300 sect temples in these prefectures; they also assigned their headquarter staff to gather funds and supplies. Rinzai Zen headquarters in Kyoto dedicated their staff to raising funds for emergency relief. The Sōtō Zen headquarters at Eiheiji reported that it mobilized clergy to accompany members of its volunteer organization Shanti International Association to travel to northeastern Japan to aid in relief efforts. Staff at the head temple of Nichirenshū, the largest sect of Nichiren Buddhism, canceled all other activities in favor of fundraising, and the central Tokyo Nichirenshū temple Jōenji offered its accommodations to students and families with young children from the disaster area needing a place to stay. It is likely that the leaders of every other traditional Buddhist denomination dedicated their staff to raising money and gathering materials for earthquake relief.

Shinto organizations also pitched in. Shinseikyō, or the National Association of Shinto Youth, immediately established a "Disaster Policy Committee" responsible for fundraising and contacting Shinto priests in the disaster area. The online Shinseikyō message board soon filled with inquiries seeking contact with Shinto clergy in shrines that could not be contacted and in some cases were later revealed to have been destroyed.[6]

Christians in Japan, who make up less than one percent of the country's population, consistently initiate successful and high-profile social welfare activities, and they leapt into action to provide relief. On March 12, mere hours after the quake and tsunami hit the Tōhoku region, the

YMCA in Kobe began soliciting relief funds; as an organization that survived the January 17, 1995 earthquake in western Japan and provided relief to residents in Kobe, they were eager to help victims of this latest natural disaster.

World Vision Japan is still gathering relief funds and is working to aid victims; Caritas Japan, the Catholic charity, is gathering donations and working with dioceses to provide support in the afflicted region; the United Church of Christ housed refugees in its Sendai churches; and the Salvation Army in Tokyo gathered money and opened its doors to commuters in Tokyo stranded by power outages and unable to take trains home.

Japan's tiny Jewish community also joined in relief efforts. The Rabbi and volunteers from Chabad Tokyo, the center for the Lubavitcher Jewish community in Japan, drove to Sendai with food and warm clothing that they distributed to refugees left without supplies or power in their homes.

"Let us hold a collective memorial"
All Japanese religious organizations also responded to the Great East Japan Earthquake with more expressly "religious" activities. Immediately following March 11 and into the weeks that followed, temples, shrines, and other facilities held prayer vigils and other services for the dead and to seek solace for victims and divine aid for a rapid recovery. Priests at the historic Shinto shrine Kasuga Taisha in Nara undertook the daunting task of chanting the *norito* (purifying prayers to the *kami*, or Japanese deities) ten thousand times to beseech Japan's native deities for aid in renewing the nation. This ritual lasts several months, and its completion is marked by a special ceremony.

One tweet on the Faith-Based Initiative Facebook wall from a young, media-savvy Nichirenshū priest named Nichibon expresses a sentiment that was doubtless shared by many concerned with the fate of those swept away by the tsunami: "The victims of this disaster had no vigils over their bodies, nor did they have funerals. Let us hold a collective memorial. There are approximately 80,000 temples in Japan; let every temple hold a vigil and funeral for the victims. It doesn't matter if the bodies have gone missing."

The Faith-Based Network also provides reports from some of Japan's many so-called new religions—groups founded in the last two centuries that have, in some cases, grown into the largest mass movements the country has ever seen. Perhaps unsurprisingly, the new religions were among the quickest organizations to mobilize their members. Unlike the "traditional" Japanese groups, they put their lay adherents to work in large numbers. Beginning March 12, Risshō Kōseikai members began assembling themselves into "Aid Brigades" to gather emergency supplies to transport into the Tōhoku region. The Shingon Buddhism-affiliated new religion, Shinnyo-en, mobilized teams from its youth volunteer organization SeRV to travel into Tōhoku to assess damage and offer relief support. In the weeks that followed, SeRV volunteers transported food and cooking supplies to small disaster-area communities not fully covered by government relief, and they even began supplying Miyagi Prefecture schools with musical instruments to replace those swept away by the tsunami. Tenrikyō, the large new religious movement based in Tenri City in western Japan, has been dispatching teams of adherents from all over Japan into the disaster zone to aid in cleanup and reconstruction. Tenrikyō maintains a practice called *hinokishin* wherein lay adherents demonstrate gratitude by taking part in public service. Since March 11, some of the most dedicated Tenrikyō adherents have practiced *hinokishin* by traveling to Tōhoku in order to dig out mud and debris and to build shelters. In addition, Tenrikyō headquarters transformed its enormous Tenri City dormitories, ordinarily used to house pilgrims traveling to its headquarters, into a refugee center for 3,000 people displaced by the disaster in the northeast.

Perhaps the largest-scale new religion disaster-response was coordinated by Sōka Gakkai, which claims 8.27 million households in Japan, including many thousands of adherents in the disaster-stricken region. The day after the earthquake, Sōka Gakkai shut down regular operations at its massive headquarters in Shinanomachi, central Tokyo, and set its thousands of employees and ordinary member volunteers to work on relief efforts.

Staff members who ordinarily run the administrative headquarters and publish the daily newspaper *Seikyō shinbun* were tasked with gathering food, blankets, portable toilets, and other supplies, which they transported north to the disaster area. In the Tōhoku area, Sōka Gakkai opened its Culture Centers to refugees; a Gakkai employee I was in touch with over email informed me that members of its Young Men's and Young Women's Divisions worked "without rest and without sleep" to help refugees, regardless of their religious affiliation. More than 3,500 refugees were housed at Culture Centers and cared for by Gakkai volunteers—including some who had lost their own homes and family members.

Is Japan really "without religion"?

The proactive responses by Japanese religious groups was not widely publicized in the Japanese media; in fact, these initiatives would surprise many in Japan who, when asked "do you have religious faith?" would respond by declaring themselves *mushūkyō*, or "without religion."

People in Japan may turn to Buddhist temples for funerals or memorials, they may visit a Shinto shrine at New Year's, and many favor Christian ceremonies for their weddings; yet, most are likely to look askance at explicit expressions of religious faith. The number of negative responses is particularly high among younger people in Japan; according to research by Kokugakuin University professor of religion Nobutaka Inoue, only ten percent of college students in Japan will affirm that they are religious.[7]

Given those numbers, one might conclude that Japan is not a religious country. But Governor Ishihara's outburst and the rapid response by religions in Japan tell a different story. The resources available within Japanese religious traditions inform Ishihara's pronouncement of the tsunami as "divine punishment," and they inspire thousands of clergy and lay adherents to devote themselves to this-worldly and transcendent salvation of suffering people.

More generally, the spirit of community, resilience, and an obstinate refusal to give up in the face of adversity speaks to the country's legacy of self-cultivation, communitarianism, and self-sacrifice in the interest of social improvement—all qualities that can be characterized as "religious." It is this legacy that will underlie the commitment of people in Japan to the rebuilding effort in the years ahead; it is this ethos that religious organizations will rely on as they progress from reacting to the immediate needs of disaster victims to the potentially more challenging task of caring for those suffering in the midst of Japan's long-term recovery.

Notes

1. Ishihara's remarks and Murai's response were reported by Kyodo News, "Ishihara apologizes for 'divine punishment' remark," *Japan Times*, March 15, 2011.
2. For a list of Robertson's statements connecting natural disasters to divine wrath over perceived moral failings, see: http://www.time.com/time/specials/packages/article/0,28804,1953778_1953776_1953771,00.html. For more on the conversation between Robertson and Falwell, see: http://www.actupny.org/YELL/falwell.html.
3. Data for the 4/10/11 election are available here: http://www.asahi.com/senkyo/local2011/data/D13.html.
4. The Facebook group (in Japanese) is accessible here: http://www.facebook.com/FBNERJ. The information that follows is drawn from reports made available on this site.
5. For the full story (in Japanese), see: http://www.asahi.com/national/update/0316/TKY201103160485_01.html.
6. Updates on Shinseikyō responses to the disaster are available here: http://www.shinseikyo.net/saigai/aska.cgi.
7. Inoue Nobutaka, *Japanese College Students' Attitudes Towards Religion: An Analysis of Questionnaire Surveys from 1992 to 2001*, Tokyo: Kokugakuin University, 2003.

CROSSCURRENTS

MAKING A SPACE FOR HOPE
Representing the Creative Reinvention of Japanese Mountain Asceticism in the Documentary Shugendō Now

Mark Patrick McGuire*

Introduction: gathering at nature's home

On April 3, 2011 at 6 A.M., 200 pilgrims from diverse backgrounds gathered at "Nature's Home" in Oguchi, Wakayama prefecture (south of Kyoto), to embark upon an introductory bout of mountain austerities undertaken for the benefit of the souls of individuals who perished in the devastating earthquake and tsunami in northeastern Japan on March 11, 2011.[1] Donning white pilgrims' robes stamped with "Hail Kumano Avatar" and protective Sanskrit script provided for the occasion by the local non-profit organization *Kumano Produce Sports*, the mixed-gender and all-ages group had arrived from the length and breadth of the archipelago (Fig. 1). These white-robed early risers had

---

*I wish to express my gratitude to Pamela Winfield for her encouragement, support, and editorial attentiveness. Her many suggestions and clarifications greatly improved the essay. Barbara Ambros' invitation to participate in a panel to honor the work of Carmen Blacker stimulated initial reflections on our filmmaking approach. I am grateful to Tanaka Riten, Tateishi Kōshō, Gojō Ryoki, Iwagishi Shinsei, Tateishi Rika, Ozaki Hitoshi, Suzuki Akiko, Miyamoto Kazuhiko, and Fujie Noritoshi for their guidance, generosity, and eloquence during filmmaking in Kumano, Yoshino, Tokyo, and Osaka. In Ibaraki, the Fujita, Kawanishi, and Ozaki families provided sustenance, outstanding company, and a tatami room to begin initial editing. In Montreal, Kory Goldberg, Matthew Penney, François Thibeault, Lynda Clarke, Donald Boisvert, and Rotem Ayalon provided encouragement and practical advice in preparing this essay for publication. Jean-Marc Abela took a chance on a risky film project in a culture and language he knew nothing about; devoted thousands of hours to film, edit, mix and discuss the film; and consistently demonstrated a great deal of creativity, sensitivity, and patience. All translations and photographs are mine unless otherwise indicated.

come seeking an authentic experience of traditional mountain ascetic practices along the well-trod Kumano pilgrimage route.

Their guide and spiritual leader on this occasion, local mountain ascetic and environmental activist Tateishi Kōshō, taught the neophyte ascetics to chant the Heart Sutra punctuated by blasts of his and his devotees' conch shells. The eight-hour event culminated in the lighting of a massive outdoor fire ritual (*saitō goma*) and a nourishing boar stew served with glutinous rice cakes. Throughout the 16-km course, participants found time for reflection and contemplation not only of Kumano's lush flora, fauna, rivers, streams, and waterfalls but also of their own interior landscapes. Concerns for family, friends, neighbors, and fellow citizens whose lives had been turned upside down and shaken violently by the force of the 9.0 scale earthquake and subsequent aftershocks were palpable.

Japan's main island of Honshu had shifted eight feet eastward since the first trembling of its tectonic plates mere weeks prior.[2] Estimates of lives lost crept upward toward 20,000 (and exceed 30,000 as I write this essay two months hence), orphaned children and elderly in northeastern communities passed uncertain evenings outdoors or in makeshift shelters as snow fell, and new cracks appeared daily in the rosy assurances of safety and security of the nation's nuclear reactors as radioactive iodine was found in Tokyo's drinking water, and radioactive cesium in

Figure 1. Prayers at Nachi Shrine to calm the souls of earthquake and tsunami victims. Photo credit: Imaizumi Eiko © 2011. Used with permission.

produce, dairy and fish from Ibaraki, Miyagi, Tochigi and Fukushima prefectures.[3] Facing up to the most severe challenges since the Second World War, pilgrims entered the Kumano mountains with uncertainty about their collective future.

Imaizumi Eiko, a female participant from Tokyo who had been learning to play the conch shell with Tateishi during monthly lessons in the metropolis over the course of the last year, expressed her surprise and delight with how many people joined the event. Most uninformed people, she assumed, would associate the mountain practices with a religious cult and consider participation too dangerous.[4] Imaizumi was also pleased when exhausted fellow pilgrims requested she play her conch shell to energize the group.[5] It was the first time she had played her conch for anyone else. Imaizumi also expressed the meaning and benefits she gained from practice at Tateishi's training site in Kumano called "The Forest of Mountain Learning."

> I feel myself at "home," where I can relax, feel safe, and at the same time, [be in] a place where I meet "myself," a self I had never known or met, but didn't want to face. (. . .) Being with the mountains, rivers, waterfalls, air, and sky, praying and playing the conch fulfills me emotionally, mentally and makes me realize that after all, I am part of this universe.

Other motivations along a spectrum of the mundane and otherworldly also inspired the pilgrims' journey: escape from boredom, sense of homecoming and rejuvenation in nature, combining austerities with a soak in Kumano's hot springs, and curiosity about the UNESCO World Heritage status of the region are found at the lighter end. At the heavier end of things, joblessness, depression, inability to settle down and move forward in life, lack of fulfillment in career and family life, substance abuse, infertility, anxiety, and trauma are some of the most common motivations lay practitioners report for pursuing engagement in mountain disciplines.[6]

Participants' goals are not always explicit or transparent, however, even to themselves. Some come looking for a chance to reconnect with nature, for spiritual and practical guidance, for assurances in whatever form available that they will hit upon the means of participating in social and economic life. Some have more clear objectives—that is, to dislodge blockages in the flow of their lives and/or offer gratitude for the intercession of powerful deities in their lives. Although none may articulate it in these terms, the crises many of them face stem from the complex interplay of personal life circumstances, societal dividing practices, and the low-grade anxiety and turmoil accompanying the dwindling prospects for future happiness, satiety, and well-being that is becoming more commonplace in contemporary Japan. Miyazaki has called this "the temporality of no hope."[7] Shut out from any means of obtaining full-time, secure employment or the means to participate fully in economic and political life, increasingly younger and younger Japanese men and women simply opt of education, training, and employment rather than face the prospects of disappointment that many feel will be their lot even after decades of hard work, study, and struggle to make it in the current climate of neoliberal economic and social reforms. Known as "NEET" (Not in Education, Employment or Training), "Freeters," (Free, part-time workers) and "parasite singles" (unmarried adult children who remain in the family home), these renunciates, like Melville's Bartleby the Scrivener, respond to pressures to conform in the neoliberal climate with a calm refusal: "I would prefer not to" (Fig. 2).

Figure 2. Tateishi's sunset address before pilgrims at Nachi Falls. Photo credit: Imaizumi Eiko © 2011. Used with permission.

Young women in particular have an especially difficult time finding their place in the post-bubble Japanese work force. Employers, often conservative older males, are reluctant to offer stable employment and a chance at upward mobility assuming young women will (or should) marry and raise a family rather than pursue careers. This is a complex and important subject deserving greater reflection than I can give it here.[8] Suffice it to say this vexing social and gendered problem, in addition to those motivations discussed above, propels a growing number of young women to participate in Shugendō practices.

Having studied this tradition and walked these mountains with diverse practitioners since 2002, and attempted to represent with my filmmaking partner Jean-Marc Abela these spaces and practices in a documentary film released in 2010, I would like to take this occasion to explore some questions that have filled me with wonder for nearly a decade now:

> What resources might a rural mountain ascetic tradition (Shugendō) provide for contemporary social, economic and ecological crisis facing the world's third largest economy in the aftermath of this monstrous trembling of the earth? Climate change, global warming, species habitat destruction and the precipitous drops in biodiversity were already on the list prior to the earthquake and tsunami. Things have since worsened.
>
> Can these emergent communities in rural and urban spaces be seen as a new social movement? If so, what kind? What deep needs within contemporary Japanese society and beyond does it satisfy?
>
> Might it be situated within efforts to find alternatives to consumer capitalism on a neo-liberal model? To what extent is the renewed interest nourished by the powerful sentiments and energies of disaffected urban youth increasingly opting out of or refused access to full-time, permanent employment and family life?

Before identifying preliminary answers to these questions I shall first provide further context in part one of this essay for understanding this place, these practices, and our interests and stake in making them the subject of our feature documentary film "Shugendō Now" (Abela & McGuire 2010).[9] In part two, I introduce our main character Tateishi

Kōshō and suggest reasons for his appeal and resonance with local practitioners and a global film audience. I engage with theoretical works from Marxist philosophy, cultural criticism, and anthropology on the concept of hope to present a framework for the analysis of Tateishi's creative reinvention of an "eco-pilgrimage" as a space of hope (Fig. 3).

Documenting the Kii Peninsula: place, practices, and concerns

I have been studying the creative reinvention of mountain ascetic practices called Shugendō, "The Way to Acquire Power," with a primary focus on its manifestations in the Kii Peninsula (Wakayama, Nara & Mie prefectures). In June 2004, the region's lush ascetic training grounds and pilgrimage route was designated a UNESCO World Heritage cultural landscape.[10] Shugendō practitioners perform ritual actions and venerate divinities from the "Shintō" kami tradition, Tantric Buddhist, Daoist and shamanistic cosmographies.[11] These divinities have been freely intermingled most of the time, but during one repressive period (Meiji: late 19th to early 20th century) an attempt was made to forcibly separate the divinities.

Figure 3. Imaginative map of the Kii peninsula. Pencil on parchment by Eric Grice© 2009.

In our documentary, we evoke the ambivalent legacies of the Meiji transition and subsequent Pacific War through a subjective, pilgrim's point-of-view and composite narrator's voice describing the experience of walking through a monocultural timber plantation. These cedar plantations (J. sugi, *Cryptomeria japonica*)[12] were part of a national campaign to replace trees "sacrificed" during rebuilding of areas devastated by American firebombing in the final months of World War II.[13] Our young female narrator describes a moment of realization in the silent factory forest. Repeated performance of the ritual practice of repentance (*sange*) and purification of the Six Roots of Perception (*rokkon shojō*)[14] enabled more acute sensory perceptions and awareness of the past that lay heavy on the landscape. She shares her realization near the film's climax:

> Abandoned rice fields have stories to share.
> Where once a community sustained itself,
> Now stands an industrial forest.
> A monoculture created by man.
> A landscape still burdened by war,
> Sixty-one cities incinerated by American bombers.
> Hungry ghosts prowl the ruins of Empire.
> It couldn't be helped.
> With fast-growing cedars
> A nation rebuilds.[15]

The practice of Shugendō was proscribed by the Meiji government, according to Shugendō priest and scholar Tanaka Riten, precisely because its syncretistic practices were perceived to undermine the imperatives of State Shintō.[16] Tanaka argues that the architects of State Shintō "brought together distorted forms of diverse local traditions to create a monotheistic tradition resembling Christianity"[17] that would, it was hoped, enable national unity and the acquisition of a global empire under the emperor as head priest. Over time, Tanaka insists, this reckless policy proved to be out of touch with daily realities of Japanese people, on the one hand, and devastating to the Japanese military, economy, society, and environment on the other.[18] Tanaka's critique is delivered in the film as voice-over narration against evocative imagery of mountain pilgrimage and the haunting *hang* drum tracks performed by Manu

Figure 4. Tanaka Riten prays to the rising sun during the Lotus Ascent of Mount Ōmine © 2007.

Delago.[19] It can and has been understood by pilgrims as both a warning against complacency and a call to revive and appreciate the value of a tradition and set of practices nearly extinguished (Fig. 4).

In the documentary, we do not provide counterpoint to Tanaka's polemic as one might in a more argumentative or expository mode of documentary storytelling, but in this essay I would like to supplement Tanaka's strident critique with reference to a more nuanced analysis of the Meiji experience at another mountain pilgrimage site. Barbara Ambros' study of Mount Ōyama (2008)[20] and the symbiotic relationship between and among its various caretakers, patrons, promoters, and pilgrims is bolstered by evidence from local archives and Japanese historiography.[21] Without such detailed examination of local primary source documents and secondary literature, Ambros claims, one might overstate the consequences of Meiji policy directives and take at face value misperceptions and stereotypes about religious institutions during this transition. Ambros names the widely repeated views that early modern Buddhist schools were essentially corrupt arms of the state[22] and that the Tokugawa military government was "unremittingly repressive."[23] Ambros' scholarship provides caution about assuming that the stated objectives and policies of the Meiji era State Shintō leaders Tanaka critiques above were applied uniformly or with equal consistency. Ambros also reveals how the Meiji state gave many institutions opportunities to operate independently and gain economic stability through local and regional partnerships such as the successful parish system established at Mount Ōyama.[24]

Participatory, ascetic filmmaking

Because of its rich, multivalent, and dramatic landscape, the Kii Peninsula is an attractive and meaningful place to visit, participate in pilgrimage and, as will be the case in this essay, think through the symbolic, affective, and pedagogic dimensions of space. I have conducted three summers of participant-observer ethnographic fieldwork (2002, 2003 & 2007) among Shugendō practitioners in the mountains as well as their home communities, work, play, and practice spaces from Hokkaido to Okinawa, Tokyo to Osaka and back again. In 2006, after having met filmmaker Jean-Marc Abela on a rooftop garden in Montreal, I invited him to accompany me to Japan in the summer of 2007, to make an ethnographic film on this place and practices. Field research and making a documentary about contemporary Shugendō practitioners brought us to mountains, caves, and waterfalls but also to French pastry shops, hostess nightclubs, karaoke boxes, concrete and extermination company headquarters, mountain top psychedelic trance parties, and even an eight-year old's piano recital. Only when my wife saw the completed film did she accept our reasons for having been in these admittedly unexpected places when she phoned from Canada.

> "I thought you were making a film about Shugendō?" she would ask.
> So did we. But it became much more.

Jean-Marc and I were intrigued by examples of participatory and self-reflexive filmmaking whereby collaborators ("subjects" in traditional ethnographic parlance) help shape the direction, approach, and content of the film and filmmakers reflect upon the impact of their presence. In one scene, for example, we see Fujie Noritoshi, an Osaka nightclub owner, cradling the camera with an extreme close-up on his face as he negotiates the steep, rocky terrain leading up to entry into the cave as womb for rebirth. Miyamoto Yasuhiko is seen carrying Jean-Marc's backpack containing his camera equipment. He kindly offered to do so enabling Jean-Marc to focus on his shots. Jean-Marc and I appear on-screen but our presence is suggestive, not central. This is not the story of two North Americans who went to Japan on our summer vacation. But as for all camera selections, sound capture, and post-production editing, sound, pacing and color correction decisions are concerned, we interject an enormous amount of subjectivity into every moment and layer of the film. How could it be otherwise?

The moment in the timber plantation discussed above is a scene where our subjective experience of the pilgrimage is most apparent. It is also the scene I am most ambivalent about and receive more mixed reactions to from viewers than any other. As an American walking the former terraced rice fields planted with fast-growing cedars to rebuild urban Japan after American firebombing campaigns, I could not help but feel somehow culpable in the silent, eerie monocultural forest whose memories lay heavy on the landscape. Although it is not my literal voice nor do I appear on-screen as witness, this scene bears my imprint and is an attempt to represent this subjective experience through cinematic language.

In general, we tried to resist the ethnographic filmic desire to explain and analyze. We do not wish to imply this expository mode is the only way ethnographic filmmaking has or can be practiced and certainly we are aware of historical and contemporary examples of exceptional, risk-taking documentary filmmaking.[25] But we thought it worthwhile to experiment with allowing content to influence form in what might be described as an "ascetic documentary."

We see ourselves as attentive but not overbearing hosts. The subtle hospitality of a Japanese tea gathering served as our model. We invite and welcome viewers, show them where to leave their shoes and freshen up, serve them a hot cup of tea and a sweet, but we do not lecture on the history of tea (or Shugendō) and point out what is displayed in the alcove (or waiting in the cave). If the viewer is attentive and curious, discoveries can be made. We have made some modest efforts to drop hints and give context but avoided the didactic mode ("This is this, this is that. . .") featured at one end of the spectrum of conventional ethnographic films. At the other is observational cinema where there is no narration or on-screen text whatsoever.[26]

With this introduction to Shugendō practices in the Kii Peninsula and our filmmaking approach in place, I next introduce Tateishi Kōshō and engage with theoretical conceptions of hope to suggest how Tateishi's new eco-pilgrimage might be understood and experienced as a space of hope by disaffected pilgrims from diverse backgrounds.

Tateishi's eco-pilgrimage as "engaged civic pedagogy" (Giroux)

> The struggle over politics and democracy is inextricably linked to creating and sustaining public spheres where individuals can be engaged as political agents equipped with the skills, capacities, and knowledge they need not only to actually perform as autonomous political agents, but also to believe that such struggles are worth taking up.[27]
>
> Henry Giroux

Tateishi Kōshō, the mountain ascetic priest who led the retreat and prayers for the earthquake and tsunami victims described above, is a fifty-six-year-old Tokyo native who relocated to Kumano twenty-five years ago to begin monastic training at the Shugendō temple Kimpusen-ji in Yoshino, Nara prefecture. Among his life experiences are an aborted career in insurance sales, a two-year stay in a Greenwich Village squat while studying modern dance at NYU, and five years bouncing around the globe as a "hippie." A gifted ocarina and conch shell player, he has recorded several CDs with African drum (djembe) accompaniment. Tateishi has established an independent temple and training lodge ("The Forest of Mountain Learning") in rural Wakayama in the shadow of the Kumano pilgrimage route mentioned above. Young women, university students, and foreigners comprise the most rapidly growing demographic at his training site, but middle school students and middle-aged pilgrims also participate. Tateishi also holds a half-day conch shell "lesson" in Tokyo every month. My first encounter with Tateishi was in July 2003 when I saw him perform with an African drumming troupe at Sakuramoto-bo temple in Yoshino, the site of a festival for world peace aligned with the Mayan ritual calendar (Fig. 5). The festival, attended by an all-ages crowd, featured amplified music in one of the dharma halls, calligraphy practice, and Zen meditation. After two energizing sets with

Figure 5. Tateishi Kōshō grooving to djembe beats, Sakuramoto-bo temple, Yoshino © 2003.

the djembe troupe, Tateishi performed a fire ritual in the temple's courtyard.

Through these activities, events, performances, and practices, Tateishi has been working to create his own sect called "Shizendō" ("The Way of Nature"), which blends aspects of Shugendō practice with yoga, ecology, art, and music. His life's work and spiritual practices arise from his criticisms of Japanese cultural chauvinism, floundering national education system, and economic exploitation of the natural environment. Each of his many interests and projects flow from his ascetic vocation, which he understands as protecting the natural environment of Kumano.

Just another eccentric?

Although the Japanese government and construction industry have effectively shut this modern ascetic out of civic-engineering projects for which charismatic predecessors such as Gyōki and Kūkai were revered,[28] Tateishi has found his calling in the remediation of damaged and polluted sites. Successful projects have included removing rusting hulks of junked cars and buses from the bed of a sacred waterfall and relocating a forty thousand tatami mat mountain.[29] Each of these projects netted him attention from local and national media outlets and enabled him to reclaim damaged training sites. Like his ascetic predecessors, Tateishi tends rice crops and offers prayers for blessings received and to guard against bad weather and pests. Authenticity and meaning should not be assumed to lie solely in the past for Tateishi and members of his eclectic community, however. Often they are busy creating new meanings to suit present and future needs of increasingly global networks, even in rural communities like Yoshino and Wakayama. Tateishi has imbibed from a store of charisma with clear precedent in Japanese religious history and continued resonance among broad sections of the Japanese population.

Were it not for his charismatic predecessors, Tateishi would be just another eccentric. An interesting and talented eccentric, yes; but would he have been able to drive away Osaka mafia by chanting sutra and forming protective mudras unless he activated recognizable sources of power with precedence and continued relevance in modern Japanese society? Would Tateishi have succeeded in mobilizing the local populace and local public office to remediate the damaged and polluted sites in the Wakayama countryside if there had been no tradition of mountain ascetics performing public works?

The combined elements of his ascetic training, personality, talents, and experiences have prepared Tateishi to fulfill this charismatic role among a global community of well-connected practitioners. But why now, why here? My hypothesis is that Tateishi and his followers constitute, in one instance, a kind of new social movement of disaffected youth, middle-aged, and elderly people who come together because of shared life experiences arising partly from the long-term economic downturn and social upheaval commonly known as the "Lost Decade" (the 1990s).[30] Having worked hard, done all that was asked of them, and still not been able to find meaningful, stable work or establish a household and family, these individuals are increasingly pessimistic about their future viability as "strong individuals" (*tsuyoi kojin*) willing to take risks (*risuku*) in neoliberal Japan (Miyazaki 2009). Quite a few find resonance with Tateishi's critiques of Japanese labor practices and education system. His simple, disciplined and engaged life, musical, spiritual, and culinary virtuosity positions Tateishi as an attractive mentor and conversation partner for those seeking answers to existential and practical questions. Rather than simply converse with individuals to diagnose what may ail them, Tateishi sends them out into the forest or, in my case, to scrub the temple's toilet, to discover the answers. He places a premium on knowledge gained from experience and contemplation of the natural and built environment, often urging visitors simply to observe and figure things out on our own. In doing so, Tateishi's example and methods might be regarded as sowing seeds of hope for a community of dropouts, down-shifters, and backsliders who may have otherwise tilled only barren fields in an eroded civil society.

Giroux: educated hope

In a recent essay titled "When Hope Is Subversive," progressive pedagogy theorist and cultural critic Henry Giroux presents a working definition and clarion call for an engaged civic pedagogy. He characterizes this civic engagement as the practice of "educated hope" and defines it as "the precondition for individual and social struggle, involving the ongoing practice of critical education in a wide variety of sites and the renewal of civic courage among citizens who wish to address social problems."[31] More than mere optimism, positive thinking, or faith in the intercession of a higher power, educated hope demands engaged struggle and is, in Giroux's estimation, a "subversive force."[32] At first glance, Giroux's formulations may appear to take us quite far afield from Kumano and Tateishi's Forest of Mountain Learning. Giroux's insights, however, do provide provocation and reminder of the primacy of public spheres as sites for authentic engagement, whether that be civic, social, cultural, or religious engagement in the public sphere. Engagement in this way offers the genuine possibility of individual and collective transformation, but only if we create and sustain vibrant public spheres in which to do it. Such possibilities are foreclosed in most private or commercial sites (shopping malls or other retail outlets, for example, and increasingly on our campuses) where our primary mode of participation is as consumers.[33] Margaret Kohn was one of the first to point out the necessity of securing public spaces lest hard-fought civil liberties and human rights be rendered moot in the absence of appropriate arenas to exercise them. In an era of chicken-wired "free speech zones" into which political protesters are corralled by police and secret service, one cannot overstate the importance of preserving every last remaining square inch of the public sphere (Fig. 6).

Figure 6. Stretching before eco-pilgrimage, Wakayama © 2007.

Significance of the landscape as a source of religious value
Kohn's and Giroux's reminder that democratic struggles are inextricably linked to the creation and sustenance of vibrant public spheres illuminates a key aspect of our investigation of ascetic Tateishi Kōshō's embodied pedagogy within the narrative and spatial frame of his eco-pilgrimage. That aspect is the *significance of the landscape as a source of religious value.* Unless and until these degraded spaces of ascetic pilgrimage are restored to viable ecosystems, Tateishi argues, the value and meaning of carrying out austerities in the Shugendō tradition are severely compromised. Moreover, pilgrims will lack hope in a future where environmental degradation and exploitation are carried out with impunity within the boundaries of a national park, cultural heritage site, and World Heritage cultural landscape. For Tateishi, central to his project of protecting and maintaining his tradition is the fierce stewardship of his local natural environment. Tateishi first underscored this vocation during a walk we took together along the pilgrimage route in 2003. Pointing to a riverbank encased in concrete and a former mountain peak smashed into gravel for highway construction, he pointedly asked, "Is this World Heritage?"[34] Rather than accept the ironies of pilgrims trekking across ancient pilgrimage routes that are now paved interstate highways or sites of dumping groups for construction waste or scrapped vehicles, Tateishi has sought to reclaim these spaces and narrate the story of their violation and remediation during mountain retreats.

I would like to further contextualize Giroux's insights into educated hope that is cultivated and practiced in the public sphere. It is situated in the tension between, on the one hand, the foreground of political engagement and struggle to reclaim the non-corporatized public spheres (what is often called "the commons"), and on the other hand, the backdrop of Japanese religious and social life, whose cultural and spiritual resonances conceive of the Japanese archipelago (and especially mountain landscapes like Kumano) as a source of religious value. Tateishi is a cosmopolitan sacred specialist whose legitimacy is rooted in his intimate knowledge and protection of the local landscape over many decades of ascetic practices and maintenance of the pilgrimage trails. In my view, his development of a modern eco-pilgrimage weaves together civic engagement in the public sphere, environmental protection, and conceptions of the land as a source of spiritual value. In efforts to untangle the complex and fine-grained motivations and meanings that novice ascetics bring on pilgrimage and which interact with Tateishi's ritual practices and spiritual teachings, I have sought to understand these practices against the backdrop of Kumano's mythic and natural landscape, which has long been the source and destination of spiritual power in Japan. Tateishi's environmentalist ethic, contemplation of the landscape, and creation and sustenance of the integrity and vitality of the physical site where practices (spiritual, cultural, political) are performed must also be given due attention. Otherwise, there can be no meaningful conception or understanding of the potential future possibilities available to novice ascetics.

Clarification of "hope as a method" (Bloch & Miyazaki)
Before applying Giroux's notion of hope as an embodied civic pedagogy to Tateishi's eco-pilgrimage, I would like to clarify and situate "hope" within a particular field. Beyond wishful thinking or religious faith anticipating a future positive outcome, Giroux and I instead draw from a lineage of German Marxist philosophers, Walter Benjamin and Ernest Bloch among them, who have sought theoretical clarification of the problem of hope. Bloch's formulations of hope lend theoretical rigor and much needed insight. Neither "something like nonsense or absolute fancy," according to Bloch, hope animates what he calls the "not-yet" (*noch nicht*) in the sense of open-ended, processual possibility. As Giroux interprets

Bloch, hope "foregrounds the crucial relationship between critical education and political agency, on the one hand, and the concrete struggles needed to give substance to the recognition that every present is incomplete, on the other."[35] Philosophy, in Bloch's estimation,[36] has been limited by its retrospective character to the task of contemplating "What has become," thus foreclosing any possibility of imagining a future of the "genuine, processively open kind."[37] Bloch's methodological shift, and this is of critical importance according to philosophical anthropologist Hirokazu Miyazaki, involves a *reorientation of the temporality of philosophy*. In other words, Bloch enables philosophers to substitute hope (a mobilizing force and not mere anticipation or wishful thinking) for contemplation as a method of engaging the world and contributing in some way toward social change.[38]

Bloch's notion of "not-yet" consciousness is the antithesis of Freud's unconscious. Miyazaki nicely states Bloch's departure as follows:

> If the power of psychoanalysis is predicated on the rebounding power of the repressed or suppressed, the power of hope as a method rests on the prospective momentum entailed in anticipation of what has not yet become.[39]

Miyazaki points out similar methodological innovations among American pragmatists like John Dewey and Richard Rorty. Philosophy becomes in their hands "an instrument of change rather than that of conservation."[40] Much, much more could be (and has been) said on this topic, but for my purposes here this preliminary discussion will suffice. As Miyazaki sees it, what is ultimately at stake in formulating hope as a method is not further theorizing, but rather the construction of an analytical framework for "apprehending concrete moments of hope" when a group of displaced urbanites in Suvavou, Fiji sought to reclaim knowledge about their past to validate claims to their dispossessed lands, their cultural authenticity, and integrity as a people.[41] Although Miyazaki's framework is of interest, I will not enunciate it here but instead limit myself to apprehending concrete moments of hope in another locale (Tateishi's eco-pilgrimage in Kumano) and suggest how such a project enables a new view of pilgrimage not as retreat or escape from "the real world," but instead constitutes an energetic confrontation and creative engagement with Japanese society's most entrenched social problems mentioned above (joblessness, depression, and so on in "the temporality of no hope").

As I would like to demonstrate, Miyazaki's mobilizing of Bloch's "not-yet" consciousness as a method of hope and reorientation of knowledge provides insights for understanding Tateishi's activities in Kumano. Below I query whether and to what extent one can apprehend concrete moments of hope in the domain of Japanese ascetics' knowledge about themselves, their tradition, and the cultural politics of environmental remediation in the present neoliberal climate that has dominated Japan's economy and society for the past few decades.

Sites of healing and transformation

In Tateishi's terms, his ascetic retreats permit novices a rare opportunity for self-reflection aimed at generating greater self-awareness and self-knowledge, the fruits of which can be positively transformative, not only for the individual but for society and the planet at the same time. More than just a gift from a knowledgeable and generous guide similar to inspiration or catharsis, hope might instead be recognized as a method for mutual reinforcement and a reminder of future possibilities available if one dares imagine them. Tateishi leads his ascetic retreats to remediated sites as a way for individuals who have grown cynical or apathetic to "see beyond the horizon of the given" (Giroux) and imagine alternative futures—futures in which one is not plagued by one or more of the conditions that initially propel pilgrims to visit Kumano mentioned at the onset of this essay. Because of the pilgrims' own vigorous participation and engaged interventions (many retreat participants have helped Tateishi haul away illegally discarded construction garbage and junked vehicles from despoiled ascetic training grounds), they generate for themselves a store of "educated hope." This enables them to imagine a future in which illicit dumping activities are no longer tolerated and the natural environment of Kumano is managed in a sustainable way for future generations of pilgrims, local residents, hikers, and other leisure seekers. Tateishi provides a space for the acquisition and performance of civic skills, self-knowledge, and hope as a method. *Embodied knowledge performed in the space of the Kumano landscape becomes transformative.* This experiential knowledge is a source and perhaps the very vehicle of hope propelling individuals toward a path of authentic agency, production, and transformation throughout their lives (Fig. 7).

Figure 7. Praying before a waterfall formerly polluted by illegal dumping © 2007.

Struggling to stay human

A twenty-six-year-old female pilgrim named Suzuki who appears in our documentary tells the story of how she quit her job in the Tokyo film industry and set out walking on the Kumano trail. An innkeeper she met encouraged her to find Tateishi's temple and stop for a night's rest. In conversation with Tateishi and fellow visitors, Suzuki reveals why she suffered an existential and physical crisis in her climate-controlled office tower. None of her colleagues or supervisors greeted her in the morning or as she departed each evening. In the heat of summer, she shivered. In winter, she could not stop sweating. She sought guidance from a friend, only to be told, "Everyone's just busy, don't worry about it."[42] This attempt at reassurance by a well-intentioned individual provoked further anxiety and suffering. As she states herself in the film,

> Even though I despised how most people around me simply endured this kind of thing by shrugging it off, I promised myself not to become this way. Instead *I struggled to be more human*, but eventually it got to the point where I could no longer maintain my balance. I quit my job. (. . .) When I collapsed due to exhaustion, it was pretty rough. Spiritually and psychologically I was

shattered. My body hurt all over, I couldn't sleep, I lost my spark. But having this happen–I guess I can say it gave me a totally transformed perspective on what I was doing and in what direction the world was moving.[43]

It was just after her recovery that we met Suzuki at Tateishi's temple. She participated with us in the eco-pilgrimage to the site of forty-seven waterfalls and stayed at the temple for one week. Following her interactions with Tateishi and other visitors, Suzuki embarked upon a journey to other recognized sites of sacred power and inspiring nature from Honshu to Hokkaido. After breaking her arm climbing a mountain on Japan's northern island, she resolved to return to her native province (Nagano) and work at a mountaineering lodge there. Suzuki eventually bought a proper pair of hiking boots to replace the Converse Chuck Taylor All Stars an innkeeper in Kumano had given her. Apparently she departed Tokyo so quickly after her recovery; she brought only a pair of sandals to walk the Kumano pilgrimage route. Since we shot the film in 2007, I have received several postcards from Suzuki expressing her satisfaction with her new job and life in the mountains and congratulating me on the birth of my son. She described how she enjoyed serving as a role model and mentor for other visitors to her lodge who have temporarily lost their way. Once or twice a year, she returns to Tateishi's temple and reconnects with him and other friends she made there. When I asked her what she felt when walking in nature, Suzuki gave this answer:

> When surrounded by nature I have a powerful sense of what it is to be human. It's a simple way of being. I return to a wonderful sensation of being neutral.[44]

I have heard a number of other pilgrims over the years describe this sensation of rejuvenation and rebirth as "becoming neutral," "being reset," or "returning to zero." Although a simple concept, its profundity and value is revealed in the embodied experience of it as truth.

Narratives of space, religious experience and hope

The retreat schedule Tateishi has devised features a sixty-hour bout of minimal water and abstention from food, hard labor maintaining the trails, visits to the sites of former illegal dumping grounds and gravel production, and producing household items out of bamboo that students take home as souvenirs. I find this a fascinating update of the traditional Shugendō pilgrimage route in which pilgrims perform prayers and make offerings at small worship sites where spirits of vanquished warriors or other local divinities had been enshrined. Sensing, perhaps, that visiting remediated natural sites and learning the narratives associated with their violation and subsequent purification would have a greater impact upon young pilgrims than, for example, the standard fare of disquieted samurai, Tateishi has assembled a thick archive filled with photographs and newspaper clippings which depict his and his followers' efforts over the past fifteen years. These new founding myths feature Osaka gangsters, dumping operations carried out under cover of night, and the heroic triumphs of local farmers who rallied around Tateishi to reclaim and purify the land. His albums contain dramatic "before and after" photographs and the machinery used to haul away rusting and rotting debris: a chartered helicopter, backhoes, dump trucks, and many helping hands. Shugendō's patron deity Fudō-myō-ō and legendary founder En no Gyōja also make appearances in these narratives, but they never overshadow the efforts of the local farmer or school lunch lady who labored to remove the garbage. Tateishi's eco-pilgrimages combine ascetic trials and environmental education, and have helped more than one man regain his health after open-heart surgery. They also offer participants the opportunity to insert themselves into the narrative by joining the ongoing struggle against shortsighted development schemes and illicit dumping raids that have contributed to Kumano's environmental crises. This comprises an effort to generate hope through the creation and sustenance of a vibrant and viable public sphere, albeit in an unexpected place—the rural context of a pilgrimage route. We can also see how Tateishi challenges pilgrims to engage with spirituality as well as ecology and politics. Although they may not have known exactly what lay in store for them prior to pilgrimage, what frequently results is that they become equipped, pace Giroux, with the requisite skills, capacities and knowledge enabling them to perform as "autonomous political agents" who believe such struggles are "worth taking up."[45]

In the time and space of Tateishi's eco-pilgrimages, participants like Suzuki report "breakthrough" moments whereby they begin to articulate previously inchoate feelings and suspicions about the source of their anxiety, anger, frustration, and aggression in the company of empathetic companions. This recalls what Tateishi characterizes as his *creation of a space for self-knowledge.* In Miyazaki's language, hope is a "reorientation of knowledge." He refers specifically to knowledge about one's past, present, and future self or community. Participants can draw confidence from ascetic trials attempted and completed. They do so in the company of new acquaintances who become a further source of prospective hope as a supportive community.

"If I can make it through this grueling weekend, pushing myself beyond what I thought I could achieve (and all the while not thinking of, for example, drugs, drink, sex, or the frustrations arising from everyday struggles)," some have realized they can then take what they learn back from the mountain to the city. Hope becomes a concrete embodiment of confidence gained, goals achieved, and a store of confidence and good will for future endeavors. Again, far from being a mere escape or retreat from participants' problems in the "real world," these eco-pilgrimages provide a welcome opportunity to face conflicts square on. The spiritual teachings, mythic backdrop, and ritual narrative structure provide not only reassurance but also a concrete method and theoretical framework for making sense of the experience. Through a modern adaptation of traditional pilgrimage and retreat practices, Tateishi accomplishes similar tasks and draws from a shared store of myth and symbolism that the Kumano ascetic guides have used for centuries in captivating pilgrims with exciting stories about cosmic or local divinities, revered warriors, and other standouts.

After teaching clients how to purify themselves in sacred waterfalls and perform ascetic disciplines along the Kumano trail, Tateishi helps participants situate their efforts to help restore the natural environment against the backdrop of Kumano's mythic landscape, thereby placing university students, farmers, office workers, night club owners, and lunch ladies within a broader narrative frame shared by these revered supernatural figures. At the same time, the struggle to clean up these degraded sites brings individuals face-to-face with their personal conflicts and dilemmas. Such efforts also bring participants in confrontation with social and institutional failures of contemporary Japanese: a corrupt government bureaucracy, pork barrel politicking that liquidates the public purse and enriches the construction industry and mafia, and widespread ignorance and apathy about the looming environmental crises facing an economy addicted to completely unsustainable nonstop growth.

In light of the recent concerns about nuclear energy production and regulation, Tateishi's analysis and embodied pedagogy would seem to offer something substantive for those struggling to deal with government and industry's lack of forthright information and apparent indifference to citizens' risks of radioactive exposure.[46] In my view, this is the kernel of Tateishi's creative reinvention of the trials in the context of environmental resistance and remediation struggles: he has created a space of hope for disaffected pilgrims from diverse backgrounds. Reflection on possible solutions and recruitment of local allies commonly follows participation at Tateishi's Forest of Mountain Learning.

Over time, participants develop their own versions of his stories about the tatami mountain or the junked Land Cruiser in the bed of a waterfall and disseminate them among each new class of newcomers. I have heard his clients describe having caught a glimpse of the buddha Fudō-myō-ō ("The Immovable One") in a waterfall or felt his reassuring presence near the end of an exhausting climb. Often the stories involve "rare" sightings of wild animals such as foxes, boars, or bears. For these urban guests, breathable air and clear night skies filled with glimmering stars nearly constitute a religious experience. Tateishi also suggests a method for sustaining this level of awareness by encouraging urban and suburban residents to seek out green spaces in their densely populated communities. Peak experiences can thus take place in the home context when pilgrims are unable to return to the mountain. In effect, Tateishi provides practical strategies for integration embedded within a non-dualistic worldview.

It is not unusual for Tateishi's adepts to pursue environmental studies, seek employment with environmentally sustainable companies, or manage in other ways to further involve themselves in the greening of their own hometowns. His updated pilgrimage and ascetic trials are a brilliant example of using the teachings to cater to the ability and interests of the student, "expedient means" (hōben) in the Buddhist idiom. Tateishi's efforts suggest the role of narrative as an embodied and experiential epistemology. Within the context of his eco-pilgrimage, we see examples of his strategies for pilgrims to implicate themselves in stories about space, religious experience, and hope, bundled together within the frame of his creative reinvention of a Shugendō mountain pilgrimage. Reaffirming what I wrote above, Tateishi conceives of his project as providing a space for pilgrims to acquire self-knowledge, an appreciation for the natural environment and some basic skills of civic engagement that have atrophied but which are getting a workout once more in twenty-first century Japan (Kingston 2006), particularly after the earthquake and tsunami. Tateishi and his students' efforts demonstrate that Shugendō is alive and relevant today.

Not all pilgrims find the practice as straightforward or immediately beneficial as it may seem from the admittedly tidy description above. Imaizumi Eiko reports her initial frustration with waking early, fasting, and embarking upon solitary walks in the mountains near Tateishi's training site as follows.

> I hated it at first—why I am here? It's only five in the morning? I had NO breakfast! I am hungry! Why am I doing this? What if I slip and fall? What if I cannot make it? What if I get lost? My leg hurts! What if, what if, what if . . . All these "thoughts" passed through me as I walked. Then I got so tired, and came to a point where I couldn't talk or think anything—but I kept walking because I had to get back. Then later, I realized how I was concentrating so much that I was there "at the moment" every step I took to walk the mountain and adjusting myself to "myself" asking, "Is this my current limit or not?" Then it wasn't so difficult to walk anymore.[47]

Through further reflection and careful placement of each footfall along the path, Imaizumi realizes that attachments to and anxieties about anticipated future outcomes prevented her from fully living in and appreciating the present (Fig. 8).

> I was always worried or complaining about the future—what MIGHT happen, and didn't pay attention so much to what is happening there "at the moment." I was always looking ahead, trying to prepare for what might come up, which is important, but without looking at what is down there where I stand. No wonder I slip

Figure 8. River, Wakayama. Photo by Jean-Marc Abela © 2007. Used with permission.

or fall! When I look back on my life, that outlined pretty much how I live in the city—I always worried about time, what people might think, what might happen, what if I did this, and that and it made me stressed out all the time. (. . .) But by experiencing it with my body—in physical motion—it made me realize more clearly how I have been.[48]

Concluding thoughts: longing for a more humane society
At the beginning of this essay, I introduced a recent prayer service and bout of mountain ascetic practices organized by a non-profit organization and attended by 200 ordinary Japanese from all walks of life. Led by Tateishi Kōshō, this encounter with Shugendō practices offered a space for reflection and hope that things will get better in the wake of the March 11, 2011 earthquake and tsunami. They prayed that citizens can count upon government and industry to share accurate information in a timely fashion, that it can put public safety ahead of stockholders' profits, and that life can resume some sense of normalcy despite the regular and legitimate warnings about the food and water supply. It is these kinds of complex, real-world problems that pilgrims confronted head on while on pilgrimage. Pilgrims' contemplation in and encounter with

nature was undertaken to generate the capacity to transform their situation in a concrete and practical sense. And their experiences in the mountains can be applied to the building of a more vibrant civil society and broader participation in social and political life.

"The longing for a more humane society," according to Giroux, ". . . does not collapse into a retreat from the world, but emerges out of critical and practical engagements with present behaviors, institutional formations, and everyday practices." Giroux and Miyazaki are not the only contemporary theoreticians to take up Bloch's notion of the not-yet consciousness. Others—among them Robert Sharp, Cornel West, Robin D. G. Kelley, and Ghassan Hage—characterize hope as "anticipatory rather than messianic, mobilizing rather than therapeutic."[49] I have tried to show how Tateishi's ascetic retreats are best understood as evidence of a longing for a more humane society. Kory Goldberg arrives at a similar realization in his intriguing work on alternative Buddhist education in Bodhgaya as a kind of pilgrimage.[50] Hope in the context Giroux describes does not ignore the anguish or pain of human suffering and exploitation, nor does it deny the complexity of social relations. Quite the contrary, writes Giroux, hope "acknowledges the need to sustain the 'capacity to see the worst and offer more than that for our consideration.'"[51] We see a similar formulation of hope in the microcosm of Kumano's landscape, World Heritage designation, and Tateishi's environmental resistance efforts and creation of an eco-pilgrimage discussed above. Hence, hope is for Giroux more than a politics; it is also a pedagogical and performative practice providing the foundation for human beings to learn about their potential as moral and civil agents.[52] This, too, resonates with what I see in Tateishi's guidance of pilgrims during ascetic trials in the Kumano countryside. Purifying oneself in a waterfall that was the former resting place of a junked Landcruiser, or swimming in a stream beside a mountain hollow where toxic construction waste previously leached into the stream and water table, pilgrims report having been inspired by Tateishi's environmental stewardship and feel compelled to offer assistance in his and others' ongoing efforts to preserve and protect ecosystems in their communities. Such engagements have proved to be restorative, hopeful in a mobilizing sense, and transformative in the lives of numerous pilgrims who have participated in his eco-pilgrimage and other ritual practices.

Notes

1. The organizers advertised the gathering as the "Event to Experience the 'Real' Kumano Pilgrimage Route," (*Kumano Kodo Honmamon Shugendo Taiken*), a name which invokes local Kansai dialect and the century's old pilgrimage trail that weaves throughout the Kumano region. Description and photographs of the event are provided by Imaizumi Eiko.
2. Harper's Index, *Harper's*, May 2011. In the same index, it was recorded that the collective force of this movement of plates generated enough energy to provide all of the energy needed to run the United States' power grid for a year.
3. Iodine-131 and cesium-137. Christine Marran, "Contamination: from Minamata to Fukushima, *The Asia-Pacific Journal*, 9:1 (May 11, 2011), pp. 1-2.
4. Personal communication by email, May 2011.
5. Ibid.
6. Personal communications from practitioners I have met during retreats and related fieldwork and filmmaking in 2002, 2003, 2007-present.
7. Hirokazu Miyazaki, 2009, "The Temporality of No Hope," In Carol Greenhouse, ed. *Personhood, Politics, Publics: New Ethnographies at the Limits of Neoliberalism*, Philadelphia: University of Pennsylvania Press.
8. One especially rich monograph examines a contingent of Japanese women who employ Western culture as a mirror to critique their own society. See Karen Kelsky, 2001, *Women on the Verge: Japanese Women, Western Dreams,* Durham, NC: Duke University Press.
9. "Shugendō Now," Montreal: Enpower Pictures, eighty-eight minutes. See http://www.shugendonow.com for further background information, scholarly and popular reviews, production stills, and a list of where the film has been screened worldwide. Two forty-two minutes classroom editions of the documentary ("Forest of Mountain Learning" and "The Lotus Ascent") with a companion study guide will be available for classroom use from the homepage beginning in August 2011.
10. For a succinct discussion of the complexities of Kii Peninsula World Heritage designation with reference to UNESCO practices worldwide and local voices of resistance, please see McGuire, 2004, "World Heritage Sites and Japanese Environmental Resistance," In Bron Taylor, *et al.*, eds., *Encyclopedia of Religion and Nature*, London: Continuum Press, pp. 1767-69. For firsthand experience and critique of designation from a UNESCO representative and Shugendō practitioner in Nikkō, Tochigi prefecture, see Harasawa Kenta, "*Sekai isan to Shugendō*" ("World Heritage and Shugendō"). *Sannō: Nikkō sangaku shugen jihō* (winter 2002), pp. 3-5. See also Harasawa's "*Sekai isan tōroku no genjitsu to igi—Nikkō to Kii no baai*" ("Meanings and Realities of World Heritage Designation—the Nikkō and Kii cases"), *Shugendō* 44 (January 2001), pp. 2-13.
11. I am aware the category of "shamanism" is highly fraught and one, not everyone, accepts outside the original context from which hallmark practices arose. Although beyond the scope of this essay, an excellent critique of the category can be found in Zeff Bjerken, "Exorcising the Illusion of Bon 'Shamans': A Critical Genealogy of Shamanism in Tibetan Religions," *Revue d'Etudes Tibetaines*, no. 6, (September 2004), pp. 4-59. Downloadable PDF is available here: http://religiousstudies.cofc.edu/about/faculty-staff-listing/bjerken-zeff.php.
12. "Japanese cedar," the conventional gloss for *sugi*, is a misnomer. The *sugi* is actually part of the cypress family.

13. Tracts composed exclusively of conifers are most common. Jonathan Knight discusses post-war reforestation campaigns and tensions between recreational forest users and forestry employees in the recent promotion of "multiple use" forests in Japan. See "From Timber to Tourism? Recommoditizing the Japanese forest." *Development and Change* 30:3 (1999), 341-359.
14. 懺悔懺悔六根清浄. What one repents (and/or reveals, has revealed) is not just individual transgressions committed in the past, but the weight of collective human suffering. One's sorrows stem from a stubborn refusal to accept the inevitability of change ("impermanence" or *mujō* 無常). When one grasps this fundamental truth of impermanence, she/he may be inspired to cease clinging to mundane passions (those which are "rooted" in the sense faculties—*rokkon* 六根 sight, hearing, taste, touch, smell and consciousness)—and strive for enlightenment. The practice of *Rokkon shōjō* calls for one to "purify" or "distance" one's self from transgressions, slippages and worldly passions, arising from illusory sensory data. These illusions obstruct the path to enlightenment. *Sange* is the meditative practice of reviewing attachments in order to delve deeper into the realization of impermanence. For an illuminating investigation of meaning and practice of *sange*, see Lucia Dolce, 2010, "The Contested Space of Buddhist Public Rituals: The *shunie* of Tōdaiji," in Michaels, Mishra, Dolce, et al. (eds.), *Grammars and Morphologies of Ritual Practices in Asia*. Wiesbaden: Harrasowitz Verlag, pp. 433-458.
15. Gitu Jain's narration written by Jean-Marc Abela and Mark Patrick McGuire. *Shugendō Now*.
16. Personal communication, Yoshino, July 2007. Tanaka is a priest at Kimpusen-ji temple in Yoshino-yama, Nara prefecture, and leads the annual "Lotus Ascent" to the peak of Mount Ōmine depicted in our documentary.
17. Ibid.
18. Ibid.
19. The *hang* drum (*hang* is German for "hand") is a percussion instrument invented in Switzerland in 2000 by Felix Rohner and Sabina Scharer of PANart. Resembling a UFO, the hang is formed from fusing two steel drums together. For further details, visit http://www.hang.org. To hear a sample of Delago's hang virtuosity, please visit http://www.manudelago.com. Both sites accessed on May 13, 2011.
20. Mount Ōyama is in the Kanto plain in what is now the outskirts of Tokyo.
21. Barbara Ambros, 2008, *Emplacing a Pilgrimage: The Ōyama Cult and Regional Religion in Early Modern Japan*, Cambridge: Harvard University Press.
22. Ibid, 239.
23. Ibid.
24. Ibid.
25. David MacDougall and Judith MacDougall's short "Under the Men's Tree" (1968/1974) is one such film that deeply marked me. Only after having lived among a group of Jie nomadic herdspeople in Uganda for 18 months without a camera did they consider themselves capable of making a fair representation. See McDougall, 1975, "Beyond Observational Cinema" in *Principles of Visual Anthropology*, Paul Hockings, ed. The Hague: Mouton, pp. 109-24, and MacDougall, 1998, *Transcultural Cinema. Selected essays* of *David MacDougall*, edited by Lucien Taylor. Princeton, NJ: Princeton University Press. For a list of all of

MacDougall's films and writings, see http://rsh.anu.edu.au/people/profile_system/public.php?id=115. Accessed 13 May 2011.

26. D.A. Pennebaker's biopic *Don't Look Back* documenting twenty-three-year old Bob Dylan's final solo acoustic concert tour of the UK in 1965 is a famous and well-studied example. See the official film page at Internet Movie Database: http://www.imdb.com/title/tt0061589. Accessed May 13, 2011.

27. Henry Giroux, 2005, "When Hope Is Subversive," In *Against the New Authoritarianism: Politics After Abu Ghraib*, Winnipeg: Arbiter Ring, p. 177. See also Giroux, 2004, "What Might Education Mean After Abu Ghraib: Revisiting Adorno's Politics of Education," in *Comparative Studies of South Asia, Africa and the Middle East*, volume 24, issue 1, pp. 5-23. Giroux takes inspiration from Theodor Adorno, 1998, "Education After Auschwitz," in *Critical Models: Interventions and Catchwords*. New York: Columbia University Press (originally presented as a radio lecture on April 18, 1966 under the title, "*Padagogik nach Auschwitz*").

28. Historian Janet Goodwin has characterized the work of these outstanding activists as "building bridges and saving souls." See her article "Building Bridges and Saving Souls: The Fruits of Evangelism in Medieval Japan," *Monumenta Nipponica* 44:2 (1989), pp. 137-149.

29. Tatami mats are woven from rice straw and are used as flooring in traditional Japanese homes. With the advent of fossil-fuel derived pesticides and fertilizers on rice crops and introduction of industrial fillers like styrofoam and polyester between the mat's layers and used as edging, these formerly biodegradable construction materials can no longer be safely or fully composted once their useful life is over.

30. This refers to the time immediately following the tanking of the economy and systematic breakdown of the postwar social structures and safety net. For signposts toward an emergent civil society in the wake of the "Lost Decade," see Jeff Kingston, 2006, *Japan's Quiet Transformation: Social Change and Civil Society in the Twenty-First Century*, London: Routledge. Tateishi's example is a case in point.

31. Ibid.

32. Giroux, 2005, p. 178.

33. Margaret Kohn, 2001, "The Mauling of Public Space," *Dissent*, 77.

34. Personal communication, Wakayama, 2003.

35. Giroux, 2005, 179.

36. Ernest Bloch, 1986 (1959), *The Principle of Hope*, trans. Neville Plaice, Stephen Plaice and Paul Knight. Cambridge: MIT Press, three volumes.

37. Miyazaki's discussion and application of ideas from Bloch's *The Principle of Hope* is contained in the introduction to Miyazaki's 2004 monograph *Hope As a Method: Anthropology, Philosophy, and Fijian Knowledge*. Durham, NC: Duke University Press, pp. 7-14.

38. Miyazaki, 2004, 14.

39. Ibid.

40. Richard Rorty, 1999, *Philosophy and Social Hope*. New York: Penguin Books, p. 29. Cited in Miyazaki, 2004, p. 15.

41. Miyazaki, 2004, 12.

42. Personal communication, Tokyo, July 2003.

43. Abela and McGuire, 2010.

44. Ibid.

45. Giroux, 2005, 177.
46. Japan's unsustainable economic growth is critiqued here: Gavan McCormack, 2001, *The Emptiness of Japanese Affluence*. New York: M.E. Sharpe. Steve Kerr, 2001, *Dogs and Demons: Tales from the Dark Side of Modern Japan*, New York: Hill and Wang, 2001.
47. Personal communication by email, Imaizumi Eiko, May 2011.
48. Ibid.
49. Giroux, 2005, 179.
50. Kory Goldberg, 2011, "Buddhists without Borders: Transnational Pilgrimage, Social Engagement, and Education in the Land of Enlightenment," Ph.D. thesis, Université de Québec à Montréal.
51. Giroux, 2005, 179.
52. Ibid.

THE CONTRACTION AND EXPANSION OF SHAMANIC LANDSCAPES IN CONTEMPORARY SOUTH KOREA

Laurel Kendall

In contemporary South Korea, shamans and clients navigate a landscape of sacred mountain space, a map that is being reconfigured by urban development, roads, congestion, and tourism but remains a sacred landscape nonetheless. I am following other anthropologists and critical geographers in their definition of "landscape" as "the meaning imputed by local people to their cultural and physical surroundings (i.e., how a particular landscape 'looks' to its inhabitants)" (Hirsch and O'Hanlon 1995, see also Basso 1996, Munn 2003). In Bender's (1993, 3) characterization, landscape is "never inert"; "[P]eople engage with it, re-work it, appropriate and contest it. It is part of the way in which identities are created and disputed, whether as individual, group, or nation-state."[1] Borrowing on the theme of the urban walker, from Baudelaire through Walter Benjamin, de Certeau (1984, 91–114) offers a particular mode of spatial contestation, describing the totalizing master plan of a city as confounded and reimagined by "walkers" on the ground whose everyday practices and superstitions are "foreign to the 'geometrical' or 'geographical' space of visual, panoptic, or theoretical construction." I will be speaking in particular of a "shamanic landscape" as the mutable stuff of visions, dreams, and spirit agency. The walkers in this

Excerpted from *Shamans, Nostalgias and the IMF: South Korean Popular Religion in Motion*, University of Hawai'i Press, 2009, and republished here with the generous permission of the University of Hawai'i Press.

chapter are shamans and gods. Their reimaginings occur among the sacred sites on Seoul's mountainous periphery and on mountainsides throughout Korea—spiritually potent rocks, springs, sön'ang trees that harbor unquiet ghosts, and—for the last twenty years or so—a proliferation of commercial shaman shrines, or *kuttang* where shamans rent space to perform their rituals. The notion of a "shamanic landscape" comes from Humphrey's (1995) analysis of Mongol history as a shifting ascendancy of fixed and legible maps and shamanic landscapes infused with the more fluid stuff of the imagination—including the agency of spirits. But where Humphrey describes a diachronic oscillation of the Mongol landscape, the contestation between urban developers' maps and shamanic visions is a contemporary South Korean dynamic, with the official mapmakers' panoptic clearly ascendant but with shamans and gods tenaciously inhabiting and reconfiguring sacred space. South Korea is a place of omnipresent displacement. Few adults live where they were born and no space is constant; seemingly in the blink of an eye, high-rise cities have replaced rice fields and villages, a common Asian story. South Korea is also a place where shamanic traditions remain strong even despite massive Christian conversions and an active Buddhist sangha. This particular excursion through a sacred landscape will hint at why this might be so.

Korean shamans (*Mansin*) and visions of tall buildings

Broadly speaking, shamans are religious practitioners who engage the spirits on behalf of the community, either through encounters during soul flight or by invoking the spirits into the here and now of a ritual space, conveying the immediacy of these experiences with their own bodies and voices.[2] While heroic male shamans have dominated the literature (Eliade 1964, Lewis 1969), a majority of Korean shamans are women. Indeed, female shamans predominate or are at least present and active in several other less well-known traditions (Tedlock 2005). The gods choose a Korean *mansin* and announce her destiny through a period of torment: ill health, madness, and other misfortune. When a woman accepts her calling, she mounts an initiation ritual in the hope that the gods will descend and open her "gates of speech" (*malmun*) so that she bursts out with inspired words from the gods and is able to perform as a *mansin*. Through visions, bodily sensations, aural cues, and intuition, she is able to convey the gods' will to clients—divining, offering advice, making effective petitions to the gods, and placating restless ancestors. Many initiations fail, and some initiates perform them several times before divine speech bursts out of them and they are recognized as true shamans.

Clients seek out a successfully initiated *mansin*, initially for divinations to determine the cause of all manner of personal and familial trouble and then, if they accept the *mansin's* diagnosis, to commission the rituals that she recommends. Korean shamans interact with gods and ancestors by divining their presence and will, by doing a variety of small rituals to placate them and sustain their favor, and by performing *kut* to feast and entertain them. *Kut*, the Korean shaman's most elaborate ritual, addresses affliction, sends ancestors to paradise, and secures blessings and prosperity for client households. More than merely incarnating the deities and the dead, *mansin* call upon the spirits' power to purify, exorcise, heal, and bring good fortune. Like many who write about these women and men in Western languages, I have called the *mansin* "shamans," doers who engage the spirits in Shirokogoroff's sense of the shaman as a "master of the spirits" not merely their vessel or "spirit medium" (1935, cited in Jakobsen 1999, xiii). In Korea "mastery" might be softened to "the ability to petition, entice, pacify, and effectively persuade the gods." Korea has a long history as a state society and the conceptualization and mode of dealing with gods reflects popular understandings of how one might treat politically powerful beings.

As a central premise of my work, the shaman's assumed ability to speak from "out there," to incorporate new material in the shape of visions or in the voices of spirits, makes shamanic traditions less an archaic survival (cf. Eliade 1964) than a dynamic domain of popular religious practice. As performance-centered rather than liturgical events, shaman rituals reveal a condition of non-fixate, open possibility (Atkinson 1989, 12). This emergent space is where, in Schieffelin's (1985) terms, the real work of ritual takes place. Shamanic practices are thus a particularly fluid, adaptable, and tenacious domain of popular religious expression. Accounts from Mongolia to the Amazon rain forest speak of shamans who act within and sometimes upon changing historical milieus, from colonization to ecological degradation.[3] And like shamanic or mediumistic practitioners in other places, Korean shamans incorporate new, sometimes radically contemporary imagery into their work (cf. Balzer 1996a,b, Humphrey 1999, Roseman 2000, 2001, Taussig 1997).

To perform *kut*, Korean *mansin* dress in the gods' costumes, invoke the gods into the here and now, and perform them into being in appropriate sequence with music and abundant offerings. Learned procedures, songs, chants, and mime structure the *kut*, but the shaman's performance also assumes an element of spontaneous possibility as the *mansin* dances and mimes manifestations of the gods and ancestors and speaks with their authority. She divines, performs dramatic play, and improvises on the basic structure of chants to mesh with the client's own situation and the immediate circumstances of the ritual. As in other kinds of improvisational performance, turns of phrase that provoke laughter and particularly effective bits of mime tend to be repeated from one performance to another and then are borrowed from one shaman to another. An assumed openness to visions and inspiration permits contemporary imagery. Chants evoke the ghosts of those who died in automobile accidents, on motorcycles, in airplanes, or—in the wake of 9/11—in skyscrapers. Gods promise that they will bring customers who pay "with cash and not credit," and a shaman's vision of raising a "building" becomes a more generally auspicious prognostication for different kinds of successful real estate endeavors such as my own purchase of a modest co-op apartment in New York. I soon came to realize that in a high-rise landscape that seems always under construction, the shamans I knew were using visions of "raising a building" as an idiom of prosperity and good fortune.

The characterization of the Korean shaman as a skilled improviser would seem to contradict Hultkrantz's (1997, 2) much cited notion of the shaman as a "conservative factor in culture" and the shaman's ritual enactments as a stabilizing source of tradition. A similar premise—that shamanic lore and shamanic rituals are something old, fragile, and in need of preservation—caused Korean shamans to be elevated as government-designated Human Cultural Treasures beginning in the 1980s. My emphasis on the emergent quality of what they do does not belie the wealth of cultural knowledge contained in Korean shaman practice, the performance skills and ritual lore required of a fully realized Korean shaman, or the wealth of cultural knowledge she must master. Like the mastery of technique that enables jazz inspiration or the body disciplines that enable a seemingly spontaneous stroke of black ink in a Zen painting, the wealth of skills—including conventions of divine speech—that a Korean shaman commands frame the sorts of new words and dramatic business that make intimate sense to clients in the here and now. They are not only immediately personal and of the moment but also consistent with the sorts of things that shamans, gods, and ancestors have been saying and doing in Korea for a very long time.

In contemporary South Korea, domestic crises, business reverses, the uncertainty of the market, and credit card debt may be the source of anxiety that sends a client to a shaman. In *kut* for clients suffering anxiety over the fate of their small businesses, the shamans/gods' songs and divinations packaged auspicious prognostications in the imagery of client enterprises. For a troubled florist, the shop tutelary god proclaimed: "Bunches of flowers are going in and out [to fill a large order], whether sitting or standing you will hear the sound of the door [opening constantly for clients]. . .Those who come in will not leave empty-handed. The luck of the XX Flower Shop will open wide." For an electrician: "Though my client goes east, west, south, and north . . . I will help so that there will be no power failure." For a family that runs a travel agency, the Official of the Vehicle (Ch'a Taegam) will "seize the front tire and seize the back tire and move the tour bus to an auspicious place."

Speaking in the voices of gods and ancestors, a skilled *mansin* gives common sense advice, provokes cathartic tears and laughter, and leaves her client feeling cleansed and lightened. In the *mansin's* words, they leave the client "with an unblocked path," her "gates of fortune have opened wide."

Mansin and mountains

Throughout her career, a *mansin* maintains a relationship with a sacred mountain and the gods who dwell there. As pure, high space between heaven and earth, mountains are places where gods readily descend and where their concentrated powers can be experienced most directly. As an initiate, a *mansin* prays on the mountain for visions that will confirm the presence and collaboration of gods who will help her in her practice. Initiates might make several pilgrimages to different and powerful mountains, praying through the dead of night for the power that will enable them to successfully complete an initiation ritual and practice as a fully realized shaman. Shamans revisit sacred mountains with clients or to periodically recharge their own inspirational batteries (one shaman shrine-keeper used this metaphor himself). The shamans with whom I worked most closely would commonly make a mountain pilgrimage before a major *kut* and always before the *kut* that they held annually to celebrate their own gods.

Because of the mountain's power, the pilgrim risks danger from pollution and other ritual lapses. Before making a mountain pilgrimage, a woman fasts from "bloody food" (meat or fish) for three days, abstains from sex, bathes in cold water, and cannot even so much as speak of menstruation or other polluting things. A birth or death in her own household or in the neighborhood is polluting and would force the postponement of a pilgrimage. So would news of a death. The sight of a smashed bug on the way would cause a pilgrim to turn back. Pilgrims should be silent on the mountain path and not complain that their feet hurt. I was told many cautionary tales before setting off at dawn for a day-long pilgrimage in 1977 to Kam'ak Mountain near the Imjin River with Yongsu's Mother, the shaman with whom I worked most closely, and two of her colleagues. After a bus trip and a taxi ride to the base of a mountain trail, we would hike all the way to the summit, making offerings at different sites along the way. We would return home tired, hungry, and muscle sore.

During my first fieldwork, the shaman Yongsu's Mother and her colleagues regarded mountains as barely accessible pilgrimage sites, albeit more accessible than these same mountains had been in their own youths when poorly shod and sometimes barefoot worshippers made excruciating journeys all the way on foot. In the 1970s, many of the mountains near the capital housed military observation posts, but Yongsu's Mother described them as wild, uninhabited, magical spaces where the gods' force was strongest and the shamans' visions the most vivid. Over the intervening years, I have made the journey to Kam'ak Mountain several times with Yongsu's Mother, and access to the mountain has become more convenient, aided by better roads and by the improved economic circumstances that enabled Yongsu's Mother to hire a cab for the journey in the 1980s and more recently, to have her son drive us all in the family SUV. The entire journey would take us only a couple of hours from start to return. Even so, Yongsu's Mother and her colleagues vest these journeys with great seriousness of purpose, observing the traditional fasts and baths and enjoining these on anyone who goes to pray with them.

Rather than a spring and a shrine tree up a mountain path, our destination since the early 1990s has been a mountain *kuttang*, a facility that rents space to shamans for rituals. Many small shrines on sacred mountains have been transformed into larger *kuttang* and many other *kuttang* have followed, sprouting up like mushrooms after the spring rain. *Kuttang*, like inns, restaurants, and wedding halls, are service enterprises. In addition to renting rooms with altar space and an appropriate configuration of god pictures, the *kuttang* staff provides vessels for the offering food; cooks the offering rice; steams the rice cake; caters meals on request; vends cigarettes, drinks, and tonics at inflated prices; and rents costumes and equipment to novice shamans who have not yet acquired their own. *Kuttang* personnel know how to fix offerings, anchor a full pig's carcass on a trident, and prepare the chopper blades for a shaman to balance on. Like other service enterprises, *kuttang* compete to offer upgraded facilities such as indoor plumbing, air conditioning, and expansive parking space. One of the *kuttang* I visited was equipped with an electric dumbwaiter for hauling offering food to shrine rooms on the upper floors of the multistory building.

While some proprietors of *kuttang* have the air of innkeepers or restaurateurs, others are shamans themselves or have strong links to the gods, whom they feel obligated to honor on a daily basis as shamans do. Although *kut* have been performed in rented shrine space since at least the late nineteenth century, mountain *kuttang* are now the predominant location for holding major shaman rituals (*kut*), a trend encouraged by recent changes in South Korean domestic space. Cramped apartments, dense urban neighborhoods, and lives lived on industrial time are not compatible with long rituals that involve steady drumming and percussion. Noise ordinances have commonly been construed by the shamans as a means of harassment that has successfully removed their activity from everyday domestic space. Holding a *kut* in a distant *kuttang* may also be more compatible with contemporary South Koreans' desire for anonymity when they air intimate family knowledge in a ritual setting, the sort of privacy that was unknown in the rural villages of generations past.

Even as commercial shaman shrines have sprung up on many South Korean mountainsides, other developments have constricted the shamans' access to once-sacred sites. The story of South Korean urban development since the 1960s has a parallel narrative in the destruction of many long-standing shrines as roads were widened and neighborhoods reconfigured. One of the shrines in my study had been relocated three times before its fourth site was leveled in the new millennium to accommodate a high-rise development. Youngsu's Mother sees all of this activity as diluting the potency of the mountains themselves:

> Today, even the sacred mountains [myŏngsan] are being stripped and leveled, stripped and leveled, to make roads, to build apartments. That's why the mountains give less inspiration now than in the past . . . The gods on the mountain used to live on the pine needles, but now they can't because the mountains are being stripped and leveled. So don't the gods just descend into human beings? . . . In the past, if you wanted to seek out a shaman, then you would have to walk twenty ri,[4] thirty ri, but nowadays, here's one, and there's one, and there's another one. They're everywhere.

In her view, the shamans of today lack the powers of their predecessors but there are more shamans now than ever before. In addition to new construction, other mountain sites have been placed off limits owing to either security restrictions or because they sit on rezoned parkland (Pak 2001, Ryu 2008). Fresh remnants of shamanic activity on some of these sites suggest resistance in the dead of night, and Mansin complain bitterly that they lack an effective advocacy community such as would protect a Christian church or Buddhist temple. But while some shrines disappear completely, others relocate to new settings, taking their name and resident gods with them. The stories of these relocated shrines—sometimes relocated multiple times—revealed the adaptive mutability of spirits to inhabit and sacralize new space. Among shrinekeepers that I interviewed, the keeper of the Fortification Shrine found her most recent site through a portentous dream, and the keeper of the Celestial Shrine found his site in Seoul because it matched a waking vision he had received while meditating at a sacred site on a distant mountain. In his survey of shrines along the Han River, Hueng-ju Pak's (2001, 108–109, 167, 182) work includes several historical and recent examples of shrines relocated with the aid of dreams. As a common motif, the gods' agency in selecting the place where they will reside recurs in the dreaming of shamans who subsequently relocate their personal shrines. The Fairy Maid, a young shaman, claimed that her divine grandfathers had helped her to secure an ideal site for her home and personal shrine under favorable rental terms in a neighborhood of other shamans and diviners near one of Korea's major universities. Yongsu's Mother described how, earlier in her career, her gods had insisted that she install them in the spare room that she was renting out to strangers. "We'll give you the rent money," they told her, making good on their promise by bringing her clients and giving her a successful practice (Kendall 1985, 56). Years later, in a splendid new bungalow, her gods insisted that she move their shrine from a side room to a more central location; in the gods' eyes, the side room was like a servants' quarters built against the side wall of the outer courtyard in a traditional Korean house.

If sacred space has shrunk in contemporary South Korea, the trajectories of individual shamans have expanded across and even beyond the South Korean landscape. As cars, vans, and mountain *kuttang* transformed the mountain pilgrimage into a convenient excursion, paved roads and national highways opened up the possibility of a relatively quick, relatively painless trip to a sacred mountain anywhere in South Korea. In the 1970s, migrants and North Korean refugees living in or near Seoul made special offerings on a mountain near their present home as a stand-in for an ancestral mountain (*ponsan*) in another part of the peninsula (ibid., 130–131). Today, Yongsu's Mother hires a van and escorts her clients to their ancestral mountain even if it is in the far south. South Korea is, after all, approximately the size of the state of New Jersey. A van loaded with shamans, clients, offerings, and ritual paraphernalia traveling after peak evening traffic can reach significant mountain sites in a few hours and return home in the early morning after a sleepless night of ritual and driving. If family claims to a native place had been reinterpreted after migration to the Seoul area, they were now being reasserted in these quick journeys to the putative and now accessible place of origin.

Where shaman traditions in Seoul enjoined initiates to make a circuit of potent mountains, this may have been a once-in-a-lifetime experience. By the 1990s, however, some of the shamans I met were describing frequent journeys from mountain to mountain to rejuvenate their own powers, journeys abetted by private cars and good roads. I met the owner of the Celestial Shrine one spring morning in 1998 when he had just returned from another pilgrimage to various mountains to revitalize his spiritual energies. His efforts had been immediately rewarded when he returned to find preparations under way for a *kut*, welcome business in that difficult spring of the so-called IMF Crisis. Oh Posal, a young Seoul-based shaman whom I interviewed over several years, made frequent mountain circuits and would soon become an international traveler. If the mountains' power is less than in the past, it has become more immediately accessible.

Tourists and shaman pilgrims

The recent history of shamanic landscapes describes not only adaptations to constriction and loss but also the reclamation of sacred sites abandoned in the disjuncture of domestic migration. Globalization and the possibility of international travel are stretching the shamans' magical map even further. On a hot August afternoon in 2003, a cranky Child God arrived unbidden at a *kut* and chased a young shaman around the offering table, angry with her because she had canceled a planned pilgrimage and deprived him of a trip to Mount Paektu, on the Chinese border with North Korea. Pilgrimages to Mount Paektu make a fitting end to this account of a transformed and still-transforming Korean shaman practice. At the apex of Korea's mountain geomancy, Mount Paektu sends energy (*ki*) through every mountain on the peninsula. As the birthplace of Tan'gun, the national ancestor and purported first Korean shaman, Mount Paektu assumes the aura of a mythic place of origin (cf. Stewart 1984, 23, Ivy 1995, 10 n. 17),[5] but for most of the second half of the twentieth century, owing to the impermeability of Cold War borders, the mountain was a distant memory to South Koreans who evoked its majesty in the first bars of their national anthem. In the 1990s, as China opened to South Korean trade, investment, and tourism, and as South Korea's democratic transformation and new prosperity conferred the mobility of package tours and more accessible passports, South Korean tourists began to visit Mount Paektu from the Chinese side.

Mount Paektu and the fantastically configured Diamond Mountains loom large in the South Korean imagination of a once and future unified Korea. In 1998, the Hyŏndae Asan Corporation, a South Korean conglomerate whose northern-born founder and heirs have espoused commitment to national reconciliation, began to offer boat tours to the Diamond Mountains, and from 2003, less expensive bus tours. Tours took place under careful control and surveillance by the North Korean hosts and with periodic breaks in service, depending on the diplomatic climate and such unforeseen mishaps as the 2008 shooting of a tourist who wandered into a restricted area. Early reports described how some among the tourists, northerners living in the South, made quiet offerings at the side of the path on behalf of ancestors and family members whose fates in the North are unknown (Kim 1998). Shamans used the opportunity of a Diamond Mountain tour to invoke the gods at the foot of the mountains and absorb their power (Kim Sung Ja, pers. comm., 12 June 2002). At the time of this writing, the Korean slopes of Mount Paektu, at least an equally potent site, remain inaccessible to organized tour groups from South Korea, but both secular tourists and shamans have been visiting the Chinese slopes for more than a decade.

English-language guidebooks on China devote little if any space to Mount Paektu, but the place has become a veritable mecca of South Korean tourism and domestic Han Chinese tourist contemplation of China's own Korean minority. Tourists scramble up to the rim of Heavenly Lake (Ch'ŏnji; Ch., Tian Chi), an enormous turquoise crater, and pose for a requisite souvenir photograph with the distant North Korean lakeshore as backdrop, then scale a steep stairway past a spectacular waterfall to the shore of the lake itself. In the early 1990s, some visitors mixed the lake water with dirt from Cheju Island, the far southernmost extension of Korea, in an act of magical reunion.

Into this transnational space, South Korean shamans make their pilgrimages, beginning with the renowned National Treasure shaman Kim Geum-hwa, who accompanied a South Korean cultural delegation to the Chinese slopes of Mount Paektu in the early 1990s and performed a *kut* for national unification. A refugee from northwestern Hwanghae Province, Kim is deeply concerned with this issue, locating her own World Shamanism Center on Kanghwa, a South Korean island across a narrow strait from northern territory. Because many shamans take Kim as a role model, it was perhaps inevitable that television broadcasts of her Mount Paektu *kut* would inspire shaman advocacy associations to organize their own public *kut* on the mountain, featuring the most renowned shamans in their membership. The Spirit Worshippers' Anti-Communist Association prominently displayed photographs and a video from their own trip in the association headquarters when I visited in 1994.

A shaman active in a rival association described her experiences when she was invited to perform at the Yanbian College of Arts in China's Korean Autonomous Region. She preceded her public *kut* with a journey up Mount Paektu to invite the gods to attend, a journey undertaken in full cognizance of the mountain's power and danger.[6] The weather was bad, but because the gods themselves had ordained the day for the ritual, she felt that she had to go, "even if it killed me." She was very much aware that three months earlier a South Korean journalist had fallen from the mountain to his death. Her hosts advised her to wear trousers for the ascent, but she insisted on wearing the full-skirted Korean costume that the gods expected; she would do things properly. Because of the weather, she and her small entourage were all alone on the mountain, and it was eerily quiet. When they reached the halfway point, the skies cleared and they had a spectacular view of the peak, a replay of the experience of the exiled eighteenth-century scholar official Sŏ Myŏngŭng when, after carefully purifying himself and performing the mountain offering with a sincere heart, he was granted not only a sudden clearing but also news of his political rehabilitation (M. Eggert, unpublished data).

When the South Korean shaman began to divine, she saw gods of both the North and the South descending from heaven to meet their counterparts. She saw good fortune pouring down on Korea. She saw a rainbow, an auspicious sign. She was reluctant to state everything the gods told her: "It wasn't as though I was doing a ritual for an individual client. Everything I said would have national implications." She did not want to risk losing face with expansive oracles recorded by a broadcast crew, but she did predict that within the next four to five years, a road would connect North and South Korea. In this, she felt vindicated because by the time of this interview in 1998, South Korean airplanes were flying over North Korea. "I was right, wasn't I?" she said with a chuckle.

These journeys, by Kim Geum-hwa and by less famous but still distinguished "great shamans" (*k'ŭn mudang*), carry the aura of cultural performance. Remarkable and remarked-upon events in the shaman's career, their public intentions, and "national implications" distinguish these journeys from the mountain pilgrimages shamans undertake either to petition the gods on behalf of clients or to recharge their own inspirational batteries. But Mount Paektu has also become the site of these more ordinary pilgrimages, like the one the young shaman had cavalierly abandoned, to the disappointment of the Child God. In 2002, I overheard a shaman team discussing during a cigarette break a forthcoming trip to Mount Paektu, one shaman complaining that she could not join the group because of her busy schedule. Could they really be talking so casually about a visit to Mount Paektu? Indeed they were, and they were not alone. I soon learned that one of the shamans I had been interviewing over several years had also been there. When I asked about journeys to Mount Paektu during another break with another group of Seoul shamans, they all treated the journey as a matter of course, pointing to one of their number who had been there "even before Kim Geum-hwa" and had subsequently gone back four more times. The shamans in these conversations represent a range of regional origins and local traditions of shaman practice, sharing the notion of numinous Korean mountains and a common recognition of the particular power of Mount Paektu.

Conclusion: the view from a distant mountain

Auspiciousness pours down on Korea from a ritual performed on Chinese territory. A Child God makes trouble when his promised trip to Mount Paektu is thwarted. With the irony of history, the permeability of post–Cold War boundaries and developments in global tourism enable shamans, with other South Korean travelers, to engage with a space they regard and experience as a quintessentially Korean site. At the same time, they vest these pilgrimages with the cachet conferred by international travel, something that successful shamans now undertake with other successful South Koreans. The mountain enables visions of unity and reconnection, but at the heart of the mountain, the view from Heavenly Lake reveals the inaccessible shore of a divided nation. Shamanic pilgrimages to Mount Paektu bespeak a global moment when gods and shamans travel routes that override national division, inhabiting an expanded and visionary landscape of "Korea" even as these same journeys underscore its complicated and still unresolved history as a divided nation. The innate instability of this site in relation to an unknown Korean future is of a piece with the notion of mutable landscapes and reconfigured sacred geographies that I have been describing here, of visionary spaces that disappear even as some others come into sharper focus, like the clouds dispelling from the peak of Mount Paektu. The manner in which shamans and gods muddle the tidy urban plans and highway grids of contemporary South Korea leads to a larger point that I have tried to affirm in most of my recent writing about Korean shamans. South Korean shamans are valorized as the bearers of traditional culture, and the repositories of music, performing arts, and ritual lore that they learn as initiates and then polish through their subsequent careers have earned them this honor. But it is as shamans, those who claim the power to enact the will of the gods, who keep visions, dreams, and spontaneous utterances an active possibility, that they have caused this distinctive spirituality to survive as something more than a museum piece. Sacred maps expand and contract, gods seek new sites and sometimes confirm them in dreams even as their words, spoken through the shamans, are uttered as immediate and resonant prognostications that sometimes draw on an imagery of tall buildings as auspicious signs. It is precisely the mutability, adaptability, and immediacy attributed to gods and ancestors, to the words they say, the visions they send, and the spaces where they choose to reside, that has enabled Korean shamanship to survive and flourish in circumstances of great social, economic, demographic, and political fluidity.

Works cited

Atkinson, Jane M., 1989, *The Art and Politics of Wana Shamanship*, Berkeley: University of California Press.

Bacigalupo, Ana M., 2004a, "Shamans' Pragmatic Gendered Negotiations with Mapuche Resistance Movements and Chilean Political Authorities," *Identities: Global Studies in Culture and Power* 11, pp. 501–41.

Bacigalupo, Ana M., 2004b, "The Struggle for Machi masculinity: Colonial Politics of Gender, Sexuality and Power in Southern Chile," *Ethnohistory* 51 (3), pp. 489–533.

Balzer, Marjorie M., 1996a, "Changing Images of the Shaman: Folklore and Politics in the Sakha Republic (Yakutia)," *Shaman* 4 (1–2), pp. 5–16.

Balzer, Marjorie M., 1996b, "Flights of the Sacred: Symbolism and Theory in Siberian Shamanism," *American Anthropologist* 98 (2), pp. 305–18.

Balzer, Marjorie M., 2001, "Healing Failed Faith? Contemporary Siberian Shamanism," *Anthropology and Humanism* 26 (2), pp. 134–49.

Basso, Keith H., 1996, *Wisdom Sits in Places: Landscape and Language Among the Western Apache*, Albuquerque: University of New Mexico Press.

Bender, Barbara, and Margot Winer, 2001, *Contested Landscapes: Movement, Exile and Place*, Oxford: Berg.

Bender, Barbara, 1993, "Introduction: Landscape—Meaning and Action," in Barbara Bender, ed., *Landscape: Politics and Perspectives*, Providence, RI: Berg, pp. 1–17.

Bender, Barbara, 2002a, "Contested Landscapes: Medieval to Present Day," in Victor Buchli, ed., *The Material Culture Reader*, New York: Berg, pp. 141–74.

Bender, Barbara, 2002b, "Landscape and Politics," in Victor Buchli, ed., *The Material Culture Reader*, New York: Berg, pp. 135–40.

de Certeau, Michel, 1984, "The Practice of Everyday Life," *Trans. Steven Rendall*, Berkeley: University of California Press.

Conklin, Beth A., 2002, Shamans Versus Pirates in the Amazonian Treasure Chest, *American Anthropologist* 104 (4), pp. 1050–61.

Eliade, Mircea, 1964, *Shamanism: Archaic Techniques of Ecstasy*, New York: Pantheon.

Hamayon, Roberte N., 1995, "Are 'Trance', 'Ecstasy' and Similar Concepts Appropriate in the Study of Shamanism?," in Mihály Hoppál, ed., *Shamanism in Performing Arts*, Budapest: Akademiai Kiado, pp. 17–34.

Hamayon, Roberte N., 1998, "'Ecstasy' or the West-dreamt Siberian Shaman," in Helmut Wautischer, ed., *Tribal Epistemologies: Essays in the Philosophy of Anthropology*, Aldershot, UK: Ashgate, pp. 175–87.

Harvey, Youngsook K., 1979, *Six Korean Women: The Socialization of Shamans*, St. Paul, MN: West Publishing Co.

Hirsch, Michael, and Eric O'Hanlon, eds, 1995, *The Anthropology of Landscape: Perspectives on Place and Space*, Oxford: Clarendon.

Hultkrantz, Ake, 1997, *Shamanic Healing and Ritual Drama: Health and Medicine in Native North America*, New York: Crossroad Publishing Co.

Humphrey, Caroline, 1995, "Chiefly and Shamanist Landscapes in Mongolia," in Michael Hirsch, and Eric O'Hanlon, eds., *The Anthropology of Landscape: Perspectives on Place and Space*, Oxford: Clarendon, pp. 135–62.

Humphrey, Caroline, 1999, "Shamans in the City," *Anthropology Today* 15 (3), pp. 3–10.

Humphrey, Caroline, and Urgunge Onon, 1996, *Shamans and Elders: Experience, Knowledge, and Power Among the Daur Mongols*, Oxford: Clarendon Press.

Ivy, Marilyn, 1995, *Discourses of the Vanishing: Modernity, Phantasm, Japan*, Chicago: University of Chicago Press.

Jakobsen, Merete D., 1999, *Shamanism: Traditional and Contemporary Approaches to the Mastery of Spirits and Healing*, New York: Berghahn Books.

Kehoe, Alice B., 2000, *Shamans and Religion: An Anthropological Exploration in Critical Thinking*, Prospect Heights, IL: Waveland Press.

Kendall, Laurel, 1985, *Shamans, Housewives, and Other Restless Spirits: Women in Korean Ritual Life*, Honolulu: University of Hawai'i Press.

Kim, Seong-wou, 1998, "A Memorable Trip to Mt. Kumgang," *Korea Focus* (November–December), pp. 88–92.

Kuchler, Susanne, 1993, "Landscape as Memory: The Mapping of Process and Representation in Melanesian Society," in Barbara Bender, ed., *Landscape: Politics and Perspectives*, Providence, RI: Berg Press, pp. 85–106.

Kuper, Hilda, 2003, "The Language of Sites in the Politics of Space," in Setha M. Low, and Denise Lawrence-Zuniga, eds., *The Anthropology of Space and Place: Locating Culture*, Cornwall, UK: Blackwell Publishers, pp. 247–63.

Lewis, I.M., 1969, *Ecstatic Religion*, Harmondsworth, UK: Penguin.

Morphy, Howard, 1993, "Colonialism, History and the Construction of Place: The Politics of Landscape in Northern Australia," in Barbara Bender, ed., *Landscape: Politics and Perspectives, Providence*, RI: Berg Press, pp. 205–43.

Munn, Nancy D., 2003, "Excluded Spaces: The Figure in the Australian Aboriginal Landscape", in Setha M. Low, and Denise Lawrence-Zuniga, eds., *The Anthropology of Space and Place: locating Culture*, Cornwall, UK: Blackwell Publishers, pp. 92–109.

Pak, Hueng-ju, 2001, *Seoulǔi Mauelgut (Seoul's Village Rituals)*, Seoul: Soemundang.

Roseman, Marina, 2000, "The Canned Sardine Spirit Takes the Mic," *World of Music* 42 (2), pp. 115–36.

Roseman, Marina, 2001, "Engaging the Spirits of Modernity: the Temiars," in Linda H. Connor, and Geoffrey Samuel, eds., *Healing Powers and Modernity: Traditional Medicine, Shamanism, and Science in Asian Societies*, Westport, CT: Bergin and Garvey, pp. 109–29.

Ryu, Je-Hun, 2008, "Kyeryong Mountain as a Contested Place," in Timothy R. Tangherlini, and Sallie Yea, eds., *Sitings: Critical Approaches to Korean Geography*, Honolulu: University of Hawai'i Press, pp. 121–40.

Schieffelin, Edward L., 1985, Performance and the Cultural Construction of Reality. *American Ethnologist* 12, pp. 707–24.

Stewart, Susan, 1984, *On longing: Narratives of the Miniature, the Gigantic, the Souvenir, the Collection*, Durham, NC: Duke University Press.

Taussig, Michael, 1997, *The Magic of the State*, New York: Routledge.

Tedlock, Barbara, 2005, *The Woman in the Shaman's Body: Reclaiming the Feminine in Religion and Medicine*, New York: Bantam.

Thomas, Nicholas, and Caroline Humphrey, eds., 1994, *Shamanism, History and the State*, Ann Arbor: University of Michigan Press.

Vitebsky, Piers, 1995b, *The Shaman: voyages of the Soul, Trance, Ecstasy and Healing from Siberia to the Amazon*, London: Macmillan Reference Books.

Notes

1. See also Bender and Winer (2001), Bender (2002a,b), Kuchler (1993), Kuper (2003), and Morphy (1993).
2. This definition is generally consistent with those provided by William P. Lebra (n.d., cited in Harvey 1979, 4), Jakobsen (1999, 3–8), and Vitebsky (1995b, 10–11) and it enables a broad ethnographic conversation. I do not hold with Alice Kehoe's (2000) suggestion, that the term "shaman" be restricted to its Siberian homeland. While acknowledging shamanic practices as vividly embodied, I have avoided the problematic and sometimes inapplicable terms "ecstasy" or "trance" (as critiqued by Hamayon 1995, 1998).
3. Bacigalupo (2004a,b), Balzer (2001), Conklin (2002), Humphrey and Onon (1996), and the several contributions to Thomas and Humphrey (1994).
4. A Chinese *li*, or Korean *ri*, equals approximately a third of an English mile.
5. While acknowledging Tan'gun, North Korea also claims Mount Paektu as the birthplace of the Dear Leader, Kim Jong Il.
6. It is a common practice to make a pilgrimage to a potent mountain or visit the shrine on a hillside behind the village before holding a *kut*.

CROSSCURRENTS
PROMINENT NUNS
Influential Taiwanese Voices

Jennifer Eichman

In recent times, scholars have certainly taken note of the burgeoning ranks of well-educated Taiwanese nuns. From the 1960s onward, the Taiwanese nuns community slowly shed its image as a vocation of the undereducated, disaffected, and lovelorn. In the last thirty years, college-educated women have swelled the ranks of well-established Buddhist monasteries and also instituted their own female enclaves. These nuns have garnered the respect of the larger society and made numerous contributions to Taiwanese social welfare, environmental protection, Buddhist education, and many other areas of social and spiritual life. The more prominent voices in this very fertile landscape have created transnational networks, increasing their global reach. As Elise DeVido has rightly pointed out, the phenomenal success of these nuns is unprecedented in the Mahayana diaspora including Korea, Japan, and Mainland China. Theravada and Tibetan communities too have yet to nurture female talent in the same sustained way.[1] In this article, I will make passing reference to the contributions of numerous talented Taiwanese nuns, while largely focusing on the work of four extraordinary individuals. They range from conservative to radically other and from studiously reflective to kinetically active.

The most internationally prominent Taiwanese nun, Cheng Yen (1937-), focuses almost exclusively on "doing religion" through charitable activities, while the nuns Kuan Ch'ien (1956-), Wu Yin (1940-), and others have made it their mission to improve the doctrinal sophistication of the sangha through education. Cheng Yen, Kuan Ch'ien, and the more politically active nun Chao Hwei (1965-), all represent a new movement in the propagation of Taiwanese/Chinese Buddhist doctrine and practice.[2] At times their approaches and organizations have been criticized, yet all three remain well within the range of contemporary normative practices. Not so for the fourth individual. Ching Hai (1950-) was tonsured in Taiwan and for a brief time she shaved her head and wore traditional monastic robes. However, she soon struck out on her own, developing what to some is Buddhist heresy and to others a new age religious organization. Without the strong financial backing and spiritual commitment of her large and loyal Taiwanese base, Ching Hai could not have severed all ties to Taiwanese Buddhist organizations and proceeded to transmit her own unique vision, let alone create an extensive global network. For this reason, I have chosen to include her here. New religious offshoots, even when they are roundly condemned by their incubating organizations, provide some comparative perspective on both what constitutes the norm and what kinds of spiritual experimentation we might expect to see from other intrepid religious innovators.

These four voices represent a range of approaches to Buddhist modernization that capitalized on Taiwan's economic advancement, female education, and democratization. The out migration of highly educated Taiwanese has been an equally indispensable factor in the ability of Taiwanese-based Buddhist organizations to create transnational networks, build temples overseas, and increase their presence in a global spiritual marketplace. Recent immigrants lend their manpower and knowledge of local laws while major Taiwanese Buddhist institutions send financial support and monastic expertise. Many institutions have also sent nuns to run these centers, thereby increasing their international visibility and educational opportunities.

Refocusing the tradition: Buddhism for the here-and-now

The twentieth century brought with it political, economic, and religious turmoil greatly hindering the ability of Mainland China Buddhist organizations to survive let alone forge creative responses to modernity.[3] This was especially so after the Communist takeover in 1949. Since the beginning of the 1982 Reform Era, Mainland Chinese have begun to revive their Buddhist institutions, yet despite the presence in Mainland China of historically famous Buddhist monasteries, these institutions have yet to achieve the global reach of such Taiwanese organizations as Compassion Relief, Dharma Drum, or Buddha's Light whose transnational networks are continually expanding operations and centers in the West and around the world.[4] In past centuries, Taiwan was a peripheral outpost that hardly warranted a dot on the map of Chinese Buddhist pilgrims and spiritual seekers. At the present moment, Taiwanese Buddhist organizations are enjoying an unprecedented newfound prominence. Compassion Relief has turned Hualian, Taiwan, into a desirable pilgrimage destination; for those seeking Buddhist instruction whether overseas Taiwanese or others, major Buddhist centers in Taiwan are prime sites for further spiritual development and academic research.

After 1949, a few Mainland monks who had fled to Taiwan slowly began to establish new forms of Buddhist practice and institutions. They were inspired by the work of the reformist monk, Taixu (1890–1947), who had promoted a human-centered Buddhist approach (*rensheng fojiao* 人生佛教). Taixu wanted Buddhists to concentrate on their role as bodhisattvas in the here-and-now rather than on rebirth in other celestial realms. He wrote extensively about the role of a socially engaged bodhisattva who was not sequestered away in a monastery, but attended to the needs of his fellow man. Much of Taixu's work was positioned to strengthen growing lay organizations, promote Buddhist participation in opening clinics, orphanages, schools, and outreach through various media such as radio and publishing.[5] Taixu called for the establishment of a Pure Land on earth. He also wrote an essay on "How to Establish Buddhism in the Human Realm (*renjian fojiao* 人間佛教)." Taixu described his vision this way, "It's a Buddhism which, in accordance with Buddhist teachings, reforms society, helps humankind to progress, and improves the whole world."[6]

In post-1949 Taiwan, Yinshun tirelessly promoted Taixu's many reformist ideas under the rubric of *renjian fojiao*. *Renjian fojiao* and the various movements inspired by it have been called humanistic Buddhism, creating an earthly Pure Land, or Buddhism for the human realm.[7] Irrespective of the nomenclature, the idea remains the same: to cultivate the bodhisattva path through selfless service to contemporary society.[8] Many Taiwanese nuns have been influenced by this movement: Cheng Yen received Yinshun's sponsorship for her ordination, and Chao Hwei and Kuan Ch'ien were both students of Yinshun. In fact, Chao Hwei often gives lectures and writes about Yinshun's ideas. Each of these nuns has further added their own imprint to what it means to develop a human-centered Buddhist practice. While this article focuses primarily on female contributions, one should not lose sight of the many contributions made by monks and nuns at Dharma Drum and Buddha's Light monasteries who have also sought to implement practices and traditions that embody the spirit of *renjian fojiao*. Because Dharma Drum, Compassion Relief, and Buddha's Light are well-endowed, large-scale organizations, they have had a profound impact on the local religious landscape. These three organizations also command the most extensive transnational networks.

However, despite the prominence of *renjian fojiao*, it must be added that there are also other successful Buddhist organizations in Taiwan that have no connection to Taixu and Yinshun's ideas, yet promote new and innovative methods of keeping Buddhism relevant to contemporary concerns. As Chao Hwei and others have said, Taiwan has a unique religious landscape wherein much of the populace has been accustomed to participating in an amalgam of Buddhist, Daoist, and popular religious God cults. Additionally, even among those who try Buddhist practice, a significant number sample different Buddhist traditions and lineages. They readily move between Theravada, Tibetan, and Chinese Buddhist centers, spending perhaps four or five years grasping the ideas of one organization or lineage master before trying another one.[9] Others, however, may settle into one community and devote all their energy to that center's mission. In general, Taiwanese Buddhist institutions do not chastise those who find religious sustenance from more than one center or master, though they do compete with each other for donations and membership.

Nuns and feminism
It has been said that behind every good man stands a good woman. In a reversal of that well-worn adage, it was powerful monks in Taiwan like Yinshun, Shengyan, and Xingyun who lent their support to nuns' ordination and education. That coupled with a relaxing of the Eight Special Precepts encoded in the Vinaya, a set of precepts that make nuns subordinate to monks, opened new leadership opportunities for nuns, and spurred the growth of an educated female cohort.[10] From the 1950s

onward, support from eminent monks spurred female advancement. In the twenty-first century, powerful nuns may well need to return the favor by recruiting more men to fill the dwindling ranks of monks.[11]

Taiwan's steady post-1949 economic gains, the lifting of martial law in 1987, the consequent rise of Buddhist groups on college campuses, the surge in female literacy, education, and rights all contributed to making it easier for women to gain a foothold in many areas of Taiwanese life, including the Buddhist *sangha*. That having been said, quite surprisingly, very few nuns attribute their success to a women's rights movement or to Western-style feminism. Rather, many powerful nuns claim that such feminine and motherly virtues as compassion, nurturance, empathy, selflessness, patience, and warmth make it easier for them to administer to others while adjusting to communal monastic life.[12] In short, many nuns follow Compassion Relief's model in praising the virtuous qualities of a traditional loving wife and mother. In contrast to societies that have tried to separate women's professional and personal lives, Taiwanese nuns view traditional nurturing skills as a professional asset that can be extended well beyond the confines of family life. Even the feminist nun Chao Hwei concedes that a "gentle feminine nature" makes women ideally suited for monastic work.[13] In what follows, I will look at some of the contributions of Cheng Yen, Chao Hwei, Kuan Ch'ien, and Ching Hai to both Taiwan's religious landscape, and where feasible, in the diaspora.

Cheng Yen and compassion relief: doing Buddhism

"It is more of a blessing to serve others than to be served." This concise statement aptly encapsulates the spirit of Compassion Relief volunteers. Whether feeding the poor, attending to nursing home occupants, or managing large-scale disaster relief missions, the typical Compassion Relief volunteer is taught that the opportunity to serve others allows for the spiritual development of the self. Service *is* practice. From the start, Cheng Yen (1937-) has followed Yinshun's directive in adhering to a program that ideally motivates her followers to manifest a bodhisattva spirit through practical action.[14] Compassion Relief, as it is commonly called, refers to a foundation whose official title is Buddhist Compassion Relief Tzu-Chi Foundation (hereafter Compassion Relief).[15] Compassion Relief has four primary missions: charitable, medical, educational, and cultural.

All four divisions and their many affiliates such as the Da'ai cable channel, and Da'ai Technology Company, LTD, are all connected through a shared sense of mission. In what follows, I will focus on the interconnection between relief missions, medical philanthropy, and efforts at environmental protection. There is a substantial, ever-growing body of English-language scholarship on Cheng Yen and her organization. Although I will draw on that material where relevant, I will not duplicate it here.[16] In comparison, Chao Hwei and Ching Hai have received scant scholarly attention in the English-speaking world, and Kuan Ch'ien is virtually unknown.

Cheng Yen's personal story and the rise of her organization from that of a small local charity to a multinational organization that by 2000 had branches in 30 countries and 5 million contributors are indeed remarkable. As it continues to grow, recent data suggest that as of 2010 Compassion Relief had an organizational presence in fifty countries and close to 10 million contributors.[17] At seventy-four years of age, this diminutive nun from a middle-class background now commands a vast network of centers known for their very professional response to disaster relief both in Taiwan and abroad. Cheng Yen is the first Taiwanese nun to have reached such prominence and stands virtually in a class all her own.[18] Since its founding in 1966, Tzu Chi Compassion Relief has constructed four state-of-the-art hospitals in Taiwan, opened a secular four-year university with a medical school, started a television channel, sent relief missions to numerous disaster areas, and established a transnational network of volunteers in fifty countries.

Cheng Yen's vision of better medical care for the poor in eastern Taiwan inspired her to build a hospital in Hualian. Against all odds and despite a series of setbacks, Cheng Yen persisted with this project, which was finally completed in 1986. Her determination propelled the organization into the limelight and shortly thereafter, financial contributions and membership exploded, rapidly doubling and then tripling the size of the organization, making it financially feasible to take on more ambitious projects and extend Compassion Relief's global reach.[19] The momentum has continued, as has Compassion Relief's ability to garner respect for its moral values, efficiency, and competence in implementing numerous projects. Compassion Relief membership numbers do, however, require some explanation. Unlike religious organizations that count members (*huiyuan* 會員) based on formal initiation or professions of faith, Compassion Relief membership figures reflect the total number of financial contributors, not active participants. There is no minimum monthly contribution: all levels of financial support are considered beneficial to the mission. To get a sense of how this works, the Cedar Grove, New Jersey branch counts 10,000 contributor-members and approximately 1,000 active participants (*zhigong*). Active participants are designated "intentional volunteers" (*zhigong* 志工) to distinguish their role from that of the commonly understood idea of an ordinary volunteer (*yigong* 義工).[20] Intentional volunteers embody a sense of religious purpose and commitment. These uniformed participants follow a designated code of conduct and transmit the ethical and cultural values of the parent organization. Their diplomatic skills, lack of (overt) proselytization, and neutral political position—disciples are told specifically not to become involved in politics or run for office—have made it possible for them to rebuild communities in Indonesia, Iran, Sri Lanka, Haiti, Mainland China, and many other places.

Compassion Relief's outreach is not haphazard but follows a rigorous set of protocols. The organization embraces modern managerial techniques, continually reassesses the outcomes of their endeavors, and seeks to constantly improve on their own efficiency, service, and effectiveness. Disaster relief is divided into three main tasks that are to be implemented in the following order: first, comfort the victims; second, ensure their physical well-being; and third, help them to return to independent living. In its current relief missions, Compassion Relief strives to arrive within the crucial first seventy-two-hour window. They send doctors and other trained medical personnel who set up medical clinics and emergency care. The communities' needs are then assessed and action is taken to restore homes, schools, and lives. Although medical personnel are on hand to deal with life-threatening problems, Tzu Chi has discovered that oftentimes earthquake victims and survivors of other disasters are in need of psychological help not physical; hence, their doctors are also trained to listen and offer emotional support.[21]

Compassion Relief does not simply distribute free food or cash payments. At every level, they invite the local community to join their efforts. For example, when first aid kits were distributed in Iran, people were instructed on their use and encouraged to share this information with others; locals in Haiti were asked to help with food distribution and other tasks. In return, they were offered free meals or small cash payments. The goal is not only to help communities recover economically but also to instill in them the Compassion Relief spirit that values helping others. This last task may indeed be hardest of all and has admittedly been met with mixed results.[22]

Doctors and nurses in Compassion Relief hospitals are aware of the organization's founding vision of compassion and service toward others. However, these hospitals embrace only the latest Western medical techniques and do not offer traditional Buddhist chanting or repentance rituals for healing, nor do they suggest as Falun Gong does that meditation can cure cancer or other illnesses.[23] Cheng Yen has encouraged the donation of cadavers for medical research, allows scientific experiments with animals, and has set up a bone marrow registry. None of this sounds particularly religious or Buddhist and has led to some criticisms that Compassion Relief is largely a secular NGO, yet the overall reverence for human life that Cheng Yen attempts to instill in everyone is woven throughout the culture of her scientific and medical organizations. This is evident in the process students are asked to follow when working with cadavers. Before the dissection of cadavers, students first pray for the deceased, post biographies of the cadavers, and after dissection, write an essay of gratitude to the donor.[24] After the cremation of the body, half the ashes are kept in a chapel where medical students can meditate and express gratitude to those who have donated their bodies. Compassion Relief does not prohibit abortion nor interfere with physician decisions. Rather, the organization's imprint is found in the level of compassionate care provided both by medical personnel and by a host of volunteers.

Compassion Relief's disaster relief work is intimately tied to its mission to protect the environment. Since at least the 1960s, recent North American Buddhist converts—like Gary Snyder, Joan Halifax, and Joanna Macy—have promoted Buddhist ecological thought, arguing that Buddhism, like Native American traditions, is closer to nature than Western Abrahamic monotheisms.[25] Critical of this view, scholars like William Bodiford and Tony Huber and others have asserted that such ideas were a fabrication of American Romanticism. In their view, neither Tibetan Buddhist nor East Asian Buddhist traditions had a particular claim to ecological mindedness nor is environmental protection inscribed in the canons of Buddhist scripture.[26] Such scholarship certainly helps us disentangle various conceptual genealogies. However, we must recognize that during the last twenty years Compassion Relief integrated environmental protection as a signature component intrinsic to all of its projects. In fact, Dharma Drum, Buddha's Light, and other Taiwanese Buddhist institutions have become major voices in the creation of a Buddhist ethos of environmental protection, energy conservation, and endorsement of green technologies. For 2011 advocates of *renjian fojiao*, the environment is of primary concern, whether conceived of as an embodied, interior realm of personal transformation or the exterior world of clean air, clean water, safe food, and the proper use of natural resources.[27]

In part because of the scale of their operations and in part because Compassion Relief is continually searching for new alternatives, environmental activists have gone on fact-finding missions to their headquarters in Hualian and other places.[28] Not only have Compassion Relief members set up more than 4,500 volunteer-staffed recycling stations in Taiwan, they have also been working to repurpose recycled materials.[29] Profits from these ventures are donated to Da'ai TV cable channel. Through the creation of its affiliate Da'ai Technology Company, LTD, members with technological expertise have produced an eco-fabric made from recycled PET bottles.[30] This material is turned into blankets that Compassion Relief distributes to disaster victims. In Thailand, Compassion Relief volunteers are working to stop coastal erosion by planting Kandelia candel;[31] in Mainland China, they have sought to recycle used glass, despite its low economic value. In 2007, Compassion Relief started an 8,000 cistern installation project in drought-prone Gansu, including the village of Ruoli. However, when this did not alleviate the water shortage in Ruoli, they agreed to relocate 210 impoverished families two hours northwest to Liuchuan, a government-designated new settlement. They helped negotiate a fair land deal with the government, built houses, designated fields, taught relocated villagers new farming techniques, and encouraged economic self-sufficiency. Relocated villagers were given houses with larger windows so that children could study by natural light.[32] After the devastating 1999 earthquake in central Taiwan, Compassion Relief rebuilt fifty schools.[33] Each school is not only earthquake resistant; buildings are also designed to reduce reliance on air-conditioning, through maximum air circulation, recycle rainwater in restrooms and minimize noise.[34] In their landscaping for the school, Compassion Relief also attended to the ecological protection of local species.[35] Compassion Relief recycles paper, plastics, electronics, and other valuable waste. Although these examples are a mere fraction of Compassion Relief's endeavors, they illustrate the range of projects and environmental concerns Compassion Relief chooses to undertake.

Cheng Yen refrains from political involvement, yet in the 1970s and 1980s she could not have built a hospital or carried out many of her projects without explicit government endorsement and help securing land.[36] After the 1987 lifting of martial law and Taiwan's development of a multi-party democratic society, Cheng Yen still refused to criticize the government, endorse candidates, campaign for structural change, or allow her followers to be politically active. Her critics believe that the kinds of large-scale social interventions needed to reverse environmental degradation, change the plight of the poor, and spur economic development require a political solution in the form of new laws, policies, and government investment. In fact without the 1995–2010 changes to environmental law and consequent government investment in recycling technology, Compassion Relief's efforts, even with its 60,000 recycling volunteers and 4,500 recycling stations, would only make a minor dent in Taiwan's overall waste management problem. Taiwan's 2002 Resource Recycling and Reuse Act and other laws have made recycling more cost-effective while spurring investment in new recycling technologies. From 1998 to 2008, Taiwan was able to increase its recycling rate to about 32 percent.[37] Americans may be surprised to learn that, by law, plastic bags are not handed out in convenience stores, 80 percent of PET bottles are recycled, and food waste is divided into two types: raw and cooked. Each type is processed and turned into animal feed or fertilizer. McDonalds, Starbucks, and other corporate entities do not leave it to the customer to recycle properly. By law, each enterprise is legally responsible for the proper sorting of plastic, paper, and food refuse generated in its establishments.

Strictly speaking, Taiwan's Buddhist organizations cannot claim sole responsibility for the improvements in Taiwan's recycling efforts. However, Compassion Relief, Dharma Drum, and Buddha's Light have all supported recycling efforts, promoted the use of non-disposable chopsticks, vegetarian diets, organic farming,[38] eco-friendly building practices, and a host of other initiatives. Environmental issues are increasingly at the forefront of efforts by these organizations to create an earthly Pure Land and realize the ideals of *renjian fojiao*.

Chao Hwei: seeking structural change

If Cheng Yen can be characterized as a soft-spoken nun who does not criticize government policies, Chao Hwei (1965-) stands as her alter ego. Convinced that structural change in the form of new government policies or the rewriting of the monastic code, the Vinaya, is the only way to effect real change, Chao Hwei has been a tireless advocate for many causes. The 2009 recipient of the "Outstanding Women in Buddhism" award,[39] Chao Hwei's prominence comes largely through her social and religious activism in Taiwan. She does not command a large monastic or lay following and thus does not oversee a global network of followers. An ethicist, university professor, and social activist, Chao Hwei uses both the journal of Hongshi Institute and the academic journal of Hsuan Chuang University as a platform for her many ideas. She has been invited to speak in Hong Kong and Mainland China and is best known among an international group of nun activists.

Chao Hwei's strident political activism and open embrace of feminism have certainly caused a stir. Her unflinching approach seen not only in her published writings but also more importantly in her very public protests against the death penalty, gambling, and nuclear power has garnered significant media attention. Chao Hwei takes credit in part for the passage of the Wild Animal Protection Law, forbidding horse racing. She has protested against the abuse of laboratory animals and advocated on behalf of a variety of animal welfare issues.[40] The causes Chao Hwei has chosen to address are far to numerous to recount here. Hence, the following discussion will be confined to the three projects Chao Hwei singled out in her "Outstanding Women in Buddhism" award acceptance speech: a 1994 "Hunger Strike to Protect Kuan-yin"; a 1999 attempt to make the Buddha's birthday a national holiday—up to that point only Christmas held that distinction; and her 2000 project "Abolishment of the Eight Special Rules for Bhikkhunis." Each of these causes demonstrates her commitment to *renjian fojiao*.

The first of these three projects propelled her into a media spotlight, resulting in both positive and negative press. Some community members who questioned the appropriateness of placing a religious image in a public space wanted a statue of the Bodhisattva Guanyin removed from the entrance to Da'an park in central Taibei. In disagreement with this perspective, Chao Hwei staged a very public protest wherein she began what was to be a six-day fast and meditation. Many monastics, accustomed to a much softer approach, criticized her bold actions as merely complicating the issue. However, the monk Xingyun stood by her, offering crucial support.[41] In this instance, Chao Hwei successfully convinced the authorities to leave the statue at the park, where it can be seen today. While this particular protest rallied for the acceptance of a religious image in a public setting, a cause that was only mildly controversial, many of Chao Hwei's other protests have championed much more sensitive and complex causes, many of which are not yet thoroughly resolved.

That in her acceptance speech, Chao Hwei would highlight her attempts to create a Buddhist holiday is somewhat puzzling. After all, this project not only failed, but it also had a negative impact on the lives of working Taiwanese. Since 1947, the twenty-fifth of December has been designated Constitution Day for the Republic of China, and thus, it was celebrated as a national holiday, not a religious one. That this was also Christmas Day was merely a fortuitous happenstance. However, the government resolved the apparent contradiction of allowing a foreign religion, Christianity, an official holiday for the birth of Christ while ostensibly ignoring the Buddha's birthday, by simply abolishing the twenty-fifth of December as a national holiday. This, of course, led to plenty of disgruntled comments by the working public, that is, the majority of Taiwanese who had previously enjoyed having the day off.

The third protest, conducted with great panache in front of TV cameras, was aimed at the long-standing Buddhist monastic practice of conferring at ordination, Eight Special Rules for nuns. From the 1960s onward, many major monasteries simply chose to disregard such rules; though, there were other monks who insisted on adherence. Well-educated nuns had not mounted protests. After all, most were reaping the fruits of a good education that allowed them to teach, travel, and participate in monastic institution building. In contrast, Chao Hwei came to the conclusion that simply ignoring these rules was not enough. She wanted them forever abolished. She felt that the dual ordination wherein nuns are ordained in front of a quorum of ten nuns and then a quorum of ten monks should also be abolished. Nuns, in her view, should only need a single ordination presided over solely by nuns. In 2000, on the eve before the Dalai Lama was to arrive in Taiwan for a discussion of nun's ordination—especially for the restoration of a nun's order in Theravada and Tibetan traditions—Chao Hwei and seven other nuns stood in front of TV cameras and slowly one by one, they tore up large sheets of paper each written with one of the eight objectionable precepts. Startling. Shocking. Yes, it was both of these, but the larger question one might pose is was it effective? This is a harder question to answer. To date, the *sangha* has not decided to rewrite the Vinaya or to expunge these rules. Many monks and nuns judged Chao Hwei's behavior at this protest and others as unbecoming of a nun. Highly visible protests aside, Chao Hwei does, however, follow her teacher Yinshun in drawing the line at running for public office.

These three incidents offer a taste of the types of activities and causes that Chao Hwei takes on in the name of *renjian fojiao*. Chao Hwei has been called a "trouble-maker" (*mafanren*), a criticism that she wears like a badge.[42] Needless to say, Chao Hwei's tactics are radically different from those of Cheng Yen. Cheng Yen demonstrates that a soft-spoken tough mindedness can effect great change. On the other hand, sharp attacks on chauvinistic monk attitudes, protests against one perceived injustice after another, and headline grabbing actions may draw needed attention to underlying problems and stimulate further discussion and awareness even if Chao Hwei cannot always elicit the outcome she so desires. In some respects, one could argue that Compassion Relief lives change while Chao Hwei advocates for it. The next nun to be discussed, Kuan Ch'ien, is a good friend of Chao Hwei. However, her approach to *renjian fojiao* differs from that of both Chao Hwei and Cheng Yen.

Kuan Ch'ien: the fine art of living well

Numerous Taiwanese nuns have completed Ph.Ds and Master's degrees, often from universities in Japan, Europe, and the United States. Many in this group are faculty at Buddhist colleges and universities. They write well-researched books, publish academic papers, and attend international conferences. However, most intellectually gifted nuns are little known outside their particular academic subfield or home monastery. Education is a time-consuming labor of love. It takes years of coursework and teaching to improve the level of Buddhist knowledge among the nuns' community and within the larger lay congregation. Several early pioneers were indefatigable proponents of nun's education. Shig Hiuwen (1912) taught at Culture University and founded the Buddhist University, Huafan when she was 76. Tianyi was also an early pioneer in the education of nuns: she drew on Buddhist claims of equality and expedient means (upāya) to argue for nun's equality.[43] More recently, Wu Yin (1940-) has dedicated herself to raising the educational level of nuns. Most of the hundred nuns at her Luminary Buddhist Institute hold postgraduate degrees. The focus at Luminary Institute is on education and scholarship, not sutra chanting, funeral rites, or charity. Although not a student of Yinshun, Wu Yin is also dedicated to creating a Pure Land on earth. However, she has chosen dharma education as the primary means to effect this change.[44]

A tireless promoter of Yinshun's ideas, Kuan Ch'ien, too strives to create a peaceful earthly Pure Land through education. Kuan Ch'ien (1956-), however, is unique in that she emphasizes the interconnectedness of three realms of knowledge: facility with doctrine and scripture, knowledge about Buddhist art and aesthetics, and the art of living a pleasing, Buddhist-centered life. Her goal is to guide her lay followers toward a Buddhist informed aesthetically pleasing way of life. In a word, her focus is on inner transformation of the self and the home. Like other nuns dedicated to a vision of *renjian fojiao*, Kuan Ch'ien promotes the bodhisattva path: her teachings largely follow those of Taixu and Yinshun. Many of her sutra lectures, in fact, draw extensively from Yinshun's publication, *Miaoyunji*. Her approach is ideally suited for educated middle-class housewives and families who want an introduction to the often arcane language of Buddhist scriptures and guidance on how to fashion a lifestyle congruent with Buddhist doctrine. Kuan Ch'ien neither promotes charitable giving as the premier method of self-cultivation as Cheng Yen has nor engage in political protests like Chao Hwei. Rather, Kuan Ch'ien is a mild-mannered nun who is admired for her gift of clear exposition and depth of knowledge about Buddhist art.

Her father Yang Yingfeng 楊英風 (1926–1997)[45] was an internationally acclaimed sculptor who had a thirty-year friendship with the nun Chueh Hsin. Chueh Hsin, too, was very interested in Buddhist arts, calligraphy, and music. After completing her bachelor's degree in architecture, Kuan Ch'ien became a disciple of Chueh Hsin. The relationship between her father and Chueh Hsin resulted in the 1988 formation of the Chueh Feng Buddhist Art and Culture Foundation. The foundation's stated purpose is the promotion of Chueh Hsin's teachings and Yang Yingfeng's artistic vision. It is also a platform for its director Kuan Ch'ien to create and promote numerous programs, foremost of which is her series of lectures on Buddhist scripture that are now available for free viewing on the foundation's website. In fact, my introduction to Kuan Ch'ien's teachings came from two Dharma Drum laywomen who have become avid watchers of her DVDs and Internet TV. Kuan Ch'ien also lectures on Buddhist art or invites scholars to do so. The more unique aspect of Kuan Ch'ien's teachings derives from her avocation of an aesthetically refined sensibility attuned to the art of living well. To this end, she sponsors exhibitions and classes on flower arranging, Buddhist art, tea drinking, and vegetarian cooking.[46] Her education in architecture has also been put to good use in rethinking spatial arrangements, especially at her education centers: for one of her centers, Chueh Feng Buddhist Study Center 覺風學苑, she created a Tang dynasty studio.

The popularity of televised cooking shows is readily apparent on Taiwan's numerous cable channels. However, Kuan Ch'ien appears to be the first nun to have developed a specifically Buddhist-oriented all-vegetarian series of cooking videos. Introduced by the nun Zhao Hui, each short episode first presents the ingredients and then explains in easy-to-follow, minute detail just how to prepare the dish. The end of the show offers a summary of the nutritional content, health benefits, and visual aesthetics of the dish. Many of the dishes are created with somewhat expensive or hard-to-find ingredients and in keeping with Buddhist strictures do not include members of the onion family or garlic. The show highlights special native plants and other ingredients found in traditional markets and Chinese cooking techniques. In other words, the shows are aimed at guiding middle-class families toward tasty, healthy, high-quality vegan diets.[47] The cooking videos are decidedly gendered: I cannot imagine a monk presiding over the same content. Without explicitly saying so, this effort promotes an alternative method of consumption: one leaves out processed and junk foods while cultivating an appreciation for indigenous local ingredients. One could surmise that this is the Taiwanese parallel to the American go local, slow food movement. Although there are currently no videos on proper tea ceremony or flower arranging, Kuan Ch'ien's centers offer such courses on a regular basis.[48]

Offering instruction in basic Buddhist scripture and doctrine; encouraging followers to learn about Buddhist art, architecture, calligraphy, sculpture and so forth; offering classes aimed at improving the quality of life by emphasizing Buddhist-oriented methods to improve one's diet, immediate environment, and leisure time activities—these and other methods are all geared toward creating a gentle, refined middle-class Pure Land. The acquisition of knowledge is a long, slow difficult process, yet Kuan Ch'ien has created numerous lecture series that patiently break down difficult doctrinal concepts through the use of visual aids, that is, diagrams and drawings, and analogies to contemporary life, and drawings on a chalkboard.[49] Kuan Ch'ien is probably the least internationally known of the nuns discussed here; however, she has lectured in Canada and Japan and established a tax-exempt foundation in California along with the American Bodhi Center in Texas.

Ching Hai: transnational new age spiritual advisor

Thus far, this article has presented three prominent nuns who, inspired by Yinshun's idea of *renjian fojiao*, have each created a unique approach to its realization. Despite their differing temperaments and strategies, all three remain within the range of acceptable monastic behavior and contemporary normative tradition. In fact, one could argue that the sheer size of Compassion Relief allows it to reshape normative Buddhism, shifting attention to matters of charity and environmental protection. Not so for Ching Hai. In the 1980s, she flirted for a brief time with the Taiwanese vocation of a nun. In 1986, Ching Hai registered her Chan Foundation with the government and drew numerous followers to her particular vision. However, according to the scholar Ding Renjie, by the early 1990s Ching Hai was at war with the Buddhist establishment. Rather than acquiesce to their demands, she cut all ties to Buddhist organizations, disrobed, grew out her hair, dressed fashionably, and set out to create her own independent "new religion."

Even by Taiwanese standards of religious self-promotion made through claims to enlightenment or command of supranormal powers, Ching Hai's blatant narcissistic refashioning resulted, with its array of eclectic costumes, spiritual fashion line seen for a short time on

European and American runways, and ever-changing hair color and styles, in a head-turning, jaw-dropping radical otherness that the majority of Taiwanese Buddhists simply could not fathom. In comparison, Chao Hwei looks like an earnest promoter of Buddhist ethics and female equality, not a radical troublemaker. Despite the controversy swirling around her, Ching Hai has been able to attract disciples in Taiwan, Malaysia, Vietnam, the United States, Europe, and to a lesser extent in many other countries. Her ambitious proselytizing efforts in Mainland China were initially quite effective, but severely curtailed in the late 1990s when the Mainland government authorities decided to ban her organization.

The twists and turns in Ching Hai's personal biography notwithstanding, a 2011 American first-time viewer of her English-language website will likely conclude that she is just another liberal New Age spiritual guru.[50] Her website declares, "Be Veg, Go Green. Save the Planet,"[51] a theme that capitalizes on growing global awareness that vegan and vegetarian diets are not only healthier but also help reduce animal cruelty and save the planet. Ching Hai's presence at climate change conferences and recent publication of books promoting her love for animals equally draws her into the global flow of recent liberal, progressive environmental activism and new age spirituality. These activities help keep this outlier in the conversational crosshairs of a broader pool of potential disciples and supporters. Ching Hai appears to have the survivor instincts of someone who knows that her relevance in the crowded, competitive world of spiritual advisors requires a media-savvy visibility and modicum of mainstream legitimacy—one that presents a futuristic vision that capitalizes on current trends without appearing too fanatical.

The media arm of her organization has moved from producing VHS tapes, to DVDs, and now internet TV. Her shows are a technologically sophisticated mix of old 1990s lectures with recent appearances. The production quality is first-rate, even if the content is not. Ching Hai's legitimacy is derived in part from a fabricated associational life, one largely facilitated through the creation of website categories that direct the reader to topics on the golden age of technology, science and religion, and so forth, through numerous web links to lectures given by other new age proselytizers of scientific or pseudo-scientific ideas. [52]

Through a careful selection of links, a spiritual guru like Ching Hai can create the façade that she is a prominent voice in the imagined on-the-ground counterpart to this cyber-world.

Ching Hai, like her nun counterparts in Taiwan, promotes a vegan/vegetarian diet. However, unlike their arguments, which are grounded in Buddhist doctrine, Ching Hai argues the case in part through a Christian-Buddhist synthesis of injunctions against killing and a more generalized appeal to karma. She also appeals to the viewer through both cyber links to video clips of "elite" vegetarians and a web long page with a long list of famous vegetarians irrespective of religious persuasion: Albert Einstein, Leonardo de Vinci, Elie Wiesel, V.S. Naipaul, and Benjamin Franklin.[53] Her link to the TED talk by Graham Hill entitled "Why I'm a Weekday Veg" also adds legitimacy. If one were surfing for a vegan restaurant or animal shelter, sites created for that subculture might also contain a link to Ching Hai's chain of Loving Hut restaurants or website.[54] Ching Hai's disciples have opened a number of vegan restaurants most notably in California, where there is considerable support for alternative lifestyles—ones that are fast becoming mainstreamed on both coasts and in more liberal cities, like Portland, Oregon. A number of Ching Hai's Vietnamese-American disciples have converted their restaurants to the Loving Hut framework. Restaurant reviews tend to give high marks for both the quality of the food and the service. The restaurants also make Ching Hai's works available to interested diners, in effect serving to spread her teachings. Her website also has a section of vegan recipes and sells a few natural food items like Organic Fair Trade Vegan European Chocolate and fake fur clothing.

In her current metamorphosis, Ching Hai makes no pretense to follow Buddhism. Her home page calls her "Supreme Master Ching Hai, a renowned humanitarian, artist, and spiritual leader (*lingxing daoshi* 靈性導師)." Ching Hai is further identified as talented in the arts and the art of living. Much of her financial support has come through the sale of her poetry, clothing line, spiritual jewelry, lamps, fans, reproductions of her paintings, and other paraphernalia. Ching Hai's spiritual shopping pages promote the idea that her jewelry will embellish the inner beauty of those who wear it. Ching Hai makes no bones about encouraging her devotees to wear beautiful clothes. Devotees often decorate their houses with the lamps and pictures that she sells. Pleasing to the eye, her paintings are of the quality one might find at JC Penneys or Wal-Mart. They are reasonably priced and fit comfortably with the aesthetic tastes of middle-class America. The jewelry, however, tends to be a mixed bag of fine pieces and kitsch and can retail in the thousands.[55] Americans accustomed to a particular Protestant view that religion and materialism are diametrically opposed, tend to find this blatant mixture of consumerism and religion rather crass. However, Asian disciples accustomed to the unremitting Buddhist calls for donations praise Ching Hai's refusal to accept monetary donations, prostrations, or gifts. There are no membership fees. Seen from this perspective, she is characterized as an ethically upright leader with a pure heart. By decorating their houses with these spiritual objects, her followers sacralize the space, turning it into a shrine to Ching Hai and her teachings. Spiritual consumption allows practitioners to feel close to a master they rarely see in person and reminds them of their commitment to this particular spiritual path.

When asked in 1993 to define her religious affiliation, Ching Hai replied, "I have explained that all religions are actually the same . . . so I include all the religions, I never taught you to attack each other's religion . . ."[56] Sometime after severing her ties with the Buddhist community and recasting herself as a spiritual guru, Ching Hai began to create a spiritual path that draws together simple religious platitudes from numerous religious traditions, yet her synthesis is primarily Christian-Buddhist with a sprinkling of Hindu ideas. In brief, the goal of the one meditation technique Ching Hai promotes, the Quan Yin method, is for the soul to return to the Kingdom of Heaven: "To meditate on God doesn't mean you worship God, it means that you become God. You realize that you and God are one."[57] This idea gestures toward the Hindu doctrine of a monistic relationship between Brahman and Atman. However, Ching Hai is more likely to cite the Bible than Hindu texts. Ching Hai also claims, following standard Chan doctrine, that everyone is the Buddha; they simply need to realize this fact. In a departure from Christian doctrine, Ching Hai claims that God is not the creator of humans; rather karmic accumulation is responsible for the repeated transmigration of the soul. In some of her videos, Ching Hai claims that "master power" or God works through her: she has been sent by (the Christian) God as his spiritual avatar (Hindu idea) or super bodhisattva (Buddhist idea) to help those on Earth. Her powers are such that when she initiates people all their past karma is eradicated. Candy and snacks she has blessed are distributed at retreats. At other times, she suggests that by cultivating the Quan Yin meditation, her practitioners can become the bodhisattva Avalokitesvara (Guanyin): "If one attains the highest level in Quan Yin practice, then one becomes like Bodhisattva Avalokitesvara, you know, Quan Yin Bodhisattva, who can hear everything, can see everything, and can help people in different corners of the universe, without having to be near them or without having to know their names or person."[58]

To be fully initiated into this practice requires adherence to a vegetarian diet and cultivation of the five Buddhist precepts: not to kill, not to lie, not to steal, no sexual misconduct, and no alcohol. Initiates are also expected to practice the Quan Yin meditation method for two and a half hours a day.[59] This particular meditation method is not part of the standard Buddhist repertoire. Rather, it appears that Ching Hai learned this method prior to her trip to Taiwan. Ching Hai grew up in Vietnam, married a German doctor, divorced him, and studied the Kirpal Light Satsang method in India with the now largely discredited Thakar Singh. The Quan Yin method is likely a modified version of the Kirpal Light methods. Ching Hai requires that one meditate on both light (guang) and sound (yin). The uninitiated are not allowed full access to the method, and the initiated are expected to keep what they know a tightly guarded secret. Without an initiation, scholars are not permitted access to group meditation.[60]

Be that as it may, a number of aspects of the practice can be gleaned from an analysis of question-and-answer sessions Ching Hai held at two retreats. Both sessions have been made publicly available on DVD. The retreats are respectively: Moon Festival Celebration held at her Florida Ashram September 26, 1999; and the Every Soul Marks Its Journey, a three-day 1998 retreat held from December 16 to 18, 1998, in Los Angeles. According to these DVDs, during the meditation process the soul detaches itself from the body and travels to heaven and back. Heaven is also described not as a literal place, but as a state of being or progressively higher levels of consciousness. Ching Hai has claimed that the mind is the secretary of the soul, that the soul chooses to let the brain know what it is doing, and that there are at least five meditative levels. She has also claimed that humans are the vibration that creates the universe and are essentially energy, that is, light and sound.

Some retreat participants voiced concern that their families were worried they had joined a cult. In fact, the accusations of cult status have been made repeatedly, especially in newspaper articles and by cult watchers. Ching Hai's response to this was simply to say that participants were free to leave at anytime. Of course, to leave is to find oneself on a slower, inferior spiritual route to ultimate liberation.[61] Such comments were about the extent of her engagement with this question: she did not offer a systematic rebuttal or equip her followers with counterarguments. Rather they were instructed simply not to engage in such discourse. In both question-and-answer sessions, Ching Hai demonstrated an easy rapport with the audience, an uncanny ability to read people, an intuitive sense of when to stop joking and pull back from sarcastic comments, and a startling irreverence for religious traditions, akin to the kinds of responses one might expect from a Chan master. Her audience did not recoil when in a response to whether she was teaching the Four Noble Truths, the Eightfold Path, and other Buddhist doctrines, Ching Hai mocked the idea that anyone needed to memorize doctrinal lists, let alone follow them. In an irreverent gesture, she pointed out that men like numbers, "Buddha he liked numbers. He's a man, I have more commonsense." And "Men are all crazy. He is no exception." But she did not stop with the Buddha: "God is a man, somehow, so he made the world in seven days. No, I'm just kidding." Such responses elicited goodhearted laughter and were not challenged.

While the audience took her comments in stride, Buddhist and Christian communities would certainly be offended by such irreverent treatment. Taiwanese Buddhist leaders not only find comments like these offensive, but harmful to their mission of raising Buddhist doctrinal literacy among their disciples. As seen in these comments, Ching Hai often makes stark gender distinctions that play with various stereotypes. On the other hand, she also calls attention to herself as a "little Asian woman no one wants to listen to."[62] In reminding her devotees of her unusual prominence, Ching Hai in effect demonstrates her ability to compete in a spiritual arena dominated largely by men. In the main, retreat participants were a very ethnically diverse group, though the majority were Asians who sat silently while others asked the questions.

Ching Hai's supporters call her Supreme Master, a name translated from the Chinese. Her detractors find this outrageous because it puts her on a par with buddhas and bodhisattvas, a level of attainment they claim she does not have. Some of her supporters even incorporate her name in the standard Chinese Buddhist recitation formula of homage to a Buddha or bodhisattva. Thus, they recite "Namo Ching Hai Wu Shang Shih." In her explanation of the name, Ching Hai presents yet another synthesis: this is not her name, but signifies that she is a daughter of the Creator, the Father, and that everyone has the name of Supreme Master.[63]

As infuriating as her persona, her materialism, and unsystematic religious synthesizing is to the Taiwanese Buddhist community and to others who have called her a cult leader, when we set aside her Buddhist roots and compare her work to that of an ever-changing array of self-made gurus, spiritual guides and newly formed religions that make up the New Age marketplace, it becomes evident that Ching Hai's work is neither the most radical nor innovative. She must compete with other gurus who also teach light and sound meditation. Narcissistic tendencies like hers are on full display on the web pages of other spiritual gurus who are essentially in the business of selling themselves: their income is generated through workshops, lectures, retreats, and the sale of books, DVDs, and other media. In this marketplace, physical appearance matters; portraits must exude an aura of spiritual wisdom. Ching Hai knows this. As she ages, it remains to be seen how she will attract the same attention. Dropping all pretense to represent Buddhism and recasting herself as a self-help guru was, for Ching Hai, a smart move. The sting of her synthesis is neutralized in the flow of a different religious current—one reserved for New Age spirituality.

Conclusion

The four remarkable voices discussed here demonstrate the pathways taken by ambitious, educated, courageous women. In fact, all four women promote the five lay Buddhist precepts, vegan diets, environmental protection, and respect for animals. Cheng Yen, Chao Hwei, and Kuan Ch'ien all found inspiration in the teachings of Yinshun, yet each chose to contribute to *renjian fojiao* in rather different ways. Cheng Yen had the foresight to build hospitals, encourage medical research, and found a charitable organization dedicated to helping disaster relief victims. Her attention to environmental issues, recycling, land reclamation, cistern distribution, energy efficiency, and other efforts have put her organization at the forefront of

Buddhist environmental activism, even if she does not call it that. Fifty years ago, America was a leader in environmental protection. However, as of 2011 Taiwan has become a world leader in reforming waste policy, enacting strict recycling laws, and encouraging technological innovation in areas related to recycling and energy. Committed to establishing a Pure Land on Earth, the Buddhist community has often developed their own initiatives. As stated earlier, Buddhists conceive of the environment as both an interior space in need of spiritual transformation and an exterior world of plants, animals, air, water, and such.

While Cheng Yen teaches that religious transformation occurs through service to others, Kuan Ch'ien has chosen to focus on the cultivation of wisdom. Her primary concern is to educate the laity. Not only is she raising Buddhist literacy, but she also offers instruction on Buddhist art and the art of living: cooking, flower arranging, and tea ceremony. On the face of it, her aesthetic interests would seem to overlap with those of Ching Hai. However, their approach to spiritual materialism is quite different. Kuan Ch'ien promotes Buddhist art, not her own creations. Nor do the lifestyles they offer overlap much beyond the promotion of vegan diets. Chao Hwei does not command either the resources or following of Cheng Yen, yet through her publications and political activism she has managed to call attention to numerous injustices both within the monastic community and without. Like Kuan Ch'ien, Chao Hwei has dedicated herself to Buddhist education and teaches college-level courses. The controversies swirling around Ching Hai should not stop us from noting just how gutsy it was for her to strike out on her own. In our continued study of Taiwanese women and their leadership within Buddhist and other religious communities, we should be open to the idea that not all female leaders will remain within the religious mainstream. Ching Hai herself seems well aware of just how religiously adventurous she has been, let us hope that for her, at least, it was somehow worth it.

Notes

1. For an overview of the status of nuns, see Nancy Barnes. 1996. Buddhist women and the nun's order in Asia. In *Engaged Buddhism: Buddhist Liberation Movements in Asia*. eds. Christopher S. Queen and Sallie B. King. Albany: State University of New York Press. Elise DeVido

points out that Taiwan's nuns enjoy more opportunities than nuns have for the past seventeen centuries. Elise DeVido. 2010. *Taiwan's Buddhist Nuns*. Albany: SUNY Press, p. 117.

2. Unlike Western scholarly publications and Mainland Chinese media, Taiwan does not use the *pinyin* system. This creates a dilemma for the researcher. Many Taiwanese have an established presence on English-language websites and in older scholarly publications with their names romanized according to this alternative system. Hence if one were looking for English-language sources on Compassion Relief and entered the *pinyin* "Zhengyan" or "Ciji," this would turn up fewer sources than if one used their preferred romanization of Cheng Yen and Tzu Chi, respectively. In the case of Zhaohui, she has indicated a preference for the continued use of Chao Hwei. Irrespective of the romanization, the Chinese characters remain the same.

3. See for example Pittman, Don A., 2001. *Toward a Modern Chinese Buddhism: Taixu's Reforms*. Honolulu: University of Hawai'i Press.

4. Scholars have yet to produce an English-language monograph devoted specifically to Dharma Drum. However, for an excellent and lengthy discussion of Buddha's Light in both Taiwan and Los Angeles, see Chandler, Stuart, 2004. *Establishing a Pure Land on Earth: The Foguang Buddhist Perspective on Modernization and Globalization*. Honolulu: University of Hawai'i Press.

5. DeVido, Elise, *Taiwan's Buddhist Nuns*, p. 95.

6. As translated and cited by Elise DeVido in, *Taiwan's Buddhist Nuns*, p. 99.

7. Elise DeVido has decided to translate this term as Buddhism for the Human Realm. Her translation is the most accurate and avoids the complications that arise with a term like "humanistic" which is at once too broad and too narrow. Her long discussion of this issue is given in *Taiwan's Buddhist Nuns*, note 1, p. 147.

8. Yinshun stressed the importance of benefiting society through adherence to a this-worldly bodhisattva path. However, he did not leave a blueprint for the precise actions anyone should take; rather he left it up to his disciples to create their own paths. For more on Yinshun's impact, see Marcus Bingenheimer, "Writing History of Buddhist Thought in the Twentieth Century: Yinshun (1906–2005) in the Context of Chinese Buddhist Historiography," *Journal of Global Buddhism* 10 (2009): 255–290.

9. There is common scholarly agreement that over at least the past hundred years, Taiwan's popular religious cults have created an amalgam of practices that draw from various aspects of the Buddhist and Daoist repertoire. Mixing of Buddhism, Confucianism, and Daoism has also gone on for centuries in Mainland China. However, over the past fifty years, a number of Buddhist and Daoist institutions have moved to disentangle their traditions from other religious expressions, creating what some scholars have called a more "canonical" Buddhism. Chao Hwei, 2006, Introduction to *Tracing the History of Cultivating the Bodhisattva Path* (ren pusa xing de lishi zulu). Taibei: Fajie Publishing, pp. 1–5.

10. DeVido, pp. 26–27.

11. According to Elise DeVido as it stands the 15,000 Taiwanese nuns comprise 75% of the monastic community. Hence despite the continued presence of an older generation of prominent male abbots, there is a perceived need to attract more male talent to the vocation. This is also likely to be a contributing factor in the stance taken by some nuns not to be overly strident in their rhetoric on the position and role of nuns. DeVido, p. 10.

12. DeVido, pp. 26, 63, 76, 89.
13. Elise DeVido, Julia Huang, Li Yuzhen, Lekshe Tsomo and many others have focused on the empowerment of nuns, their relation to feminism and social standing *vis a vis* monks, monastic ordination, and leadership roles. According to Li Yuzhen nuns legitimate their monastic identity without openly challenging patriarchal society—doing it, not demonstrating for it. As cited in DeVido, p. 26.
14. My interview on May 14, 2011 with a Compassion Relief volunteer in Cedar Grove, NJ. See also Huang, p. 213.
15. The names can be confusing: The Compassion Relief Merit Society (Ciji gongde hui) is another name for the Buddhist Compassion Relief Tzu-Chi Foundation (*fojiao ciji jijinhui*). Many branches of Compassion Relief are officially registered as NGOs. Still Thoughts Abode is a medium-sized nunnery with a residential population that hovers around a hundred. Cheng Yen's residence is here. The nunnery is economically self-sufficient and does not accept donations. Cheng Yen does not conceive of herself or the nuns as a traditional "field of merit," thus all donations are given directly to the foundation.
16. C. Julia Huang's 2009 publication, *Charisma and Compassion* nicely presents Cheng Yen's biography, the history of Compassion Relief, the structure of the organization, and several case studies of Compassion Relief communities. Elise DeVido also offers extensive coverage in her 2010 work, *Taiwan's Buddhist Nuns*. This section draws on that material but has a slightly different emphasis. I also did some interviewing of my own at a Compassion Relief branch (*fenhui*) in Cedar Grove, New Jersey in May of 2011 and will present those findings where relevant.
17. I have not seen precise data on these figures. They are claims made by the organization and not confirmed independently. David Schak was informed that Compassion Relief does not subtract the names of those who stop donating. Hence these figures perhaps better reflect the number of people who have made at least a one-time contribution. David C Schak, 2009,"Community and the New Buddhism in Taiwan," *Journal of Chinese Ritual, Theatre, and Folklore* 163 (2009.03) 169.
18. Even *Time* Magazine has taken notice of her power and influence by including Cheng Yen in "The 2011 Time 100" list.
19. For this history see, C. Julia Huang. 2009. *Charisma and Compassion: Cheng Yen and the Buddhist Tzu Chi Movement*. Cambridge: Harvard University Press, p. 194.
20. In this respect, their volunteer work and continued presence in the organization is founded on a commitment to a set of religious ideals. While some participants may choose the organization because it has a good reputation, like the Red Cross, UNICEF, or World Vision, longstanding intentional volunteers acculturate new arrivals and see to it that each mission meets the goals of the organization in both spirit and substance. In general, volunteers do not see their work as primarily a means to network or keep busy during an economic downturn as was often suggested in advice columns for the newly unemployed American after the 2008 economic downturn.
21. http://tw.tzuchi.org/en/index.php?option=com_content&view=article&id=363%3Abam-iran-earthquake (accessed May 17, 2011).
22. Among disenfranchised local populations accustomed to surviving on handouts, planting the idea that they can help each other has not been easy. In my interview with Tzu Chi

volunteers they said that Tzu Chi attempted to transmit a culture of volunteerism and generosity and offered the Haitian example. Compassion Relief does not generally work to convert recipients to Buddhism, or make them bodhisattvas committed to establishing an earthly Pure Land, rather they work to leave behind a more generalized understanding of the value of helping each other to create a better life, that is, the culture and spirit of their organization. This also makes it easier to minimize their presence and to monitor continued work and support.

23. There are numerous religious specialists in Taiwan who offer various techniques for exorcising demons and ghosts, amulets for bodily protection, and medically unproven cures for whatever ails one. Tzu Chi does not encourage any of these practices. Another new religion, Falun Gong also makes claims that its methods can cure a variety of illnesses. See David Ownby. 2008. *Falun Gong and the Future of China*. Oxford; New York: Oxford University Press.

24. Richard Madsen. 2008. Religious renaissance and Taiwan's modern middle classes, In *Chinese Religiosities: Afflictions of Modernity*. Berkeley: University of California Press, pp. 313–314.

25. There are a number of Buddhists converts who have linked the thought of American Transcendentalists like Emerson and Thoreau, Native American ideas, and Zen Buddhism: Gary Snyder and Jon Kabat-Zinn are probably the best known. Unlike scholars who have gotten caught up in trying to define true Buddhism, I do not have a problem with such creative syntheses as long as we recognize that they are in fact new and innovative approaches that do not directly reflect centuries of Asian Buddhist practice.

26. The claim that canonical Buddhist literature did not advocate environmental protection rests in part on the idea that environmental protection is a new Western idea and in part on a literal reading of the canon *sans* hermeneutics. There are certainly Hong Kong Buddhist groups that have used canonical stories to bolster their claims for a Buddhist response to environmental degradation. See for example, the many articles in Yok-shiu Lee and Alvin Y. So., eds. 1999. *Asia's Environmental Movements: Comparative Perspectives*. Armonk, N.Y.: M.E. Sharpe; William Bodiford. 2008. Buddhist ecological thought and action in North America. In *Eco-Philosophy* 2 (2007): 11-31. Published by the Transdisciplinary Initiative for Eco-Philosophy, Tōyō University; Toni Huber. 1997. Green Tibetans: A brief social history. In *Tibetan Culture in the Diaspora*. Edited by F. J. Korom. Vienna: Verlag der Österreichischen Akademie der Wissenschaften, pp. 103-119; Kenneth Kraft. The greening of Buddhist practice. In *Cross Currents*, 44.2 (Sum94): 163–180.

27. Some readers may feel that I am slighting the contributions of Dharma Drum, Buddha's Light, Fuzhi, and many other Taiwanese organizations that have also sought to protect Taiwan's environment. However, these other organizations are simply beyond the scope of my current topic: the contributions of prominent nuns to contemporary Buddhist practice.

28. Latest prominent visitor, Steven Rockefeller.

29. The Taiwan government publication, *Taiwan Review*, has a number of articles on Taiwanese environmental law and recycling efforts. Compassion Relief, its intentional volunteers, and affiliates are featured in some stories. See the following article for information on Compassion Relief's recycling efforts, eco-fabric, and the overall impact of recycling laws

on Taiwan's waste management. Kelly Her, "Creating a Sustainable Homeland," March 1st, 2010, *Taiwan Review.* http://taiwanreview.nat.gov.tw (accessed May 12, 2011).

30. Compassion Relief members are not the only ones in Taiwan looking to turn PET bottles into fabric. The Taiwanese competition to create innovative new ways to use recycled materials is actually quite stiff. What's more, their prices cannot compete with those of Mainland China. However, Taiwanese products are more likely to have been genuinely constructed from recyclables. Compassion Relief has some advantages in that its recycling harvest comes mainly from the work of an army of volunteers and does not have the same financial restraints of for-profit recycling operations. See for example, Oscar Chung. Fabrics Go Green. In *Taiwan Review* March 1, 2010.

31. A mangrove plant, Kandelia candel, is an ideal choice for the restoration of coastal wetlands. "Saving the Coast by Planting More Plants," Article from Buddhist Compassion Relief Tzu Chi Foundation. Database online. Search Global Activities at http://tw.tzuchi.org/en/ (accessed May 13, 2011).

32. Tu Xin-Yi. Tzu Chi Laiyao Village, Nov. 1, 2010. http://tw.tzuchi.org/en (accessed 5.14.2011)

33. After typhoon Morakot, Compassion Relief helped relocate an aboriginal village of the Bunung to Minzu village, Namasia township. Because the Bunung were Christian, Compassion Relief replicated the four churches that had previously stood at the town center. In keeping with Cheng Yen's philosophy of helping everyone irrespective of creed, race, or nationality, Compassion Relief has been willing to reconstruct churches, attend interfaith services, and work with those of other faiths. See, Master Cheng Yen visits church in village for typhoon survivors, Feb 2, 2010. Article from Buddhist Compassion Relief Tzu Chi Foundation. Database on-line. Search Global Activities @ http://tw.tzuchi.org/en/index. (accessed 5.14.2011)

34. Compassion Relief built earthquake-resistant schools in Sichuan after the disastrous 2008 earthquake there. They are also looking to build earthquake-resistant schools in Haiti. For Haiti, Compassion Relief has been experimenting with how to create cost effective prefabricated housing that can be assembled in just three to four days. In this respect, they are a driving force in alternative building technology, repurposing of recycled materials, and simple, functional, housing design.

35. Elise DeVido has written extensively about this mission, called Project Hope. See her work for a more extensive discussion of how Compassion Relief implements their vision. DeVido, pp. 49–63.

36. For this history see C. Julia Huang, *Charisma and Compassion*, pp. 32, 187–189.

37. Kelly Her, "Creating a Sustainable Homeland," March 1, 2010, *Taiwan Review*. http://taiwanreview.nat.gov.tw (accessed May 12, 2011).

38. Fuzhi (福智) focused on organic farming. Demand by consumers caused them to expand their operations and open a store that sells organic produce, readymade foods, and organic clothes. They have also been working with lotus farmers to lessen the use of pesticides and herbicides—a real problem in Taiwan.

39. Venerable Bhikkhuni Rattanavali is the founder of the Outstanding Women in Buddhism Awards Committee. She lives in Thailand and has held award ceremonies each year since 2002. Cheng Yen was a 2002 recipient. Anywhere from eleven to twenty awards are

given each year to nuns and lay leaders. http://www.owbaw.org/index.html#. (accessed May 12, 2011).

40. DeVido, pp. 102–105.

41. For a discussion of this see, Huang Jiashu 黃家樹. Reflections on *renjian fojiao* 人間佛教的省思. 12.2001 lecture in Hong Kong. In *Lin Kok Quarterly Journal* 蓮覺叢書 13 (7.2004) Database on-line. http://www.buddhistdoor.com/download/data3.html (accessed May 5, 2011)

42. Chao Hwei is criticized as much if not more by the monastic community than the wider public. Many find her tactics abrasive and worry that her work will damage the sangha's reputation as a whole. However, Chao Hwei's own press release characterizes her as a *"mafanren."* I suspect that finding oneself in a swirl of controversy keeps Chao Hwei and her views in the limelight and draws needed press to her causes. In fact, her actions are calculated to grab headlines, not offer timid inoffensive suggestions. http://ccbs.ntu.edu.tw/formosa/people/2-zhao-hui.html (accessed May 17, 2011).

43. DeVido, pp. 19–20, 16, 81.

44. For more information, see their website: http://www.gaya.org.tw. See also DeVido, pp. 79–91. Wu Yin and Luminary Buddhist Institute are the subject of a forthcoming monograph by Chun-fang Yu and will not be commented on further here.

45. Known in the art world as Yuyu Yang, several of his pieces are on display at the Grounds for Sculpture, Hamilton, NJ. In reference to one of his New York installations, Yang commented that: "My sculptures in general, and stainless steel sculptures in particular, harmonize man and his environment spiritually, mentally, and physically; this is why I call my sculptures lifescapes instead of environmental sculptures." As cited at http://www.groundsforsculpture.org/c_yyang.htm, quoting Charles A Riley. 1995. *Simply Put, The Subtle Sculptural Language of Yuyu Yang*. Taipei: Yuyu Yang Lifescape Sculpture Museum np. 95, p. F12.

46. Many Buddhist centers offer classes on flower arranging and other soft arts. However, I am unaware of any other organization that has put together a systematic introduction to vegetarian cooking through video production.

47. It must be noted that traditional Chinese/Taiwanese cooking did not incorporate dairy products, hence the vegan quality of the diet is not a conscious choice but a *de facto* result of adhering to more traditional dishes and methods. Dairy products are now readily available in Taiwan, though many Chinese are lactose intolerant.

48. All of Kuan Ch'ien's shows are at this site: http://cftv.chuefeng.org.tw/cf_vodindex.asp (accessed May 12, 2011).

49. In fact, because her production staff has found it very difficult to transfer her previous VCD lectures into a DVD and internet TV format, she is re-taping those lectures in front of a live audience.

50. http://www.godsdirectcontact.org (accessed May 1, 2011).

51. http://www.suprememastertv.com/vegetarian-restaurants-association-members/ (accessed May 14, 2011).

52. Her numerous TV shows can be accessed here: http://suprememastertv.com/ (accessed May 14, 2011).

53. http://al.godsdirectcontact.org.tw/vg-vip/query/index.php (accessed May 15, 2011).

54. Animal lovers such as Marian Hailey have added citations from Ching Hai's teachings and links to her site. http://www.marianhaileymoss.com (accessed May 10, 2011). It is not clear to me whether the Loving Hut restaurants are a franchise from which Ching Hai reaps a substantial income as one critic suggested. It has also been suggested that her devotees volunteer their labor, thus bringing down the operational costs. http://lovinghut.us/ (accessed May 11, 2011).

55. Critics suggest that the stated price of these items is in fact not the actual price. Devotees are apparently asked to pay up to three times the asking price. I have not been able to verify this claim, but add it here to demonstrate that there are some concerns.

56. http://www.godsdirectcontact.org/eng/faq.txt (accessed May 16, 2011).

57. Excerpt from the article, "Why Must People Be Vegetarian" http://www.godsdirectcontact.org/eng/booklet/vegetarian.html (accessed May 11, 2011).

58. http://www.godsdirectcontact.org/eng/faq.txt (accessed May 3, 2011).

59. In the last ten years, Ching Hai has developed a less rigorous way to participate. One can agree to keep a vegetarian diet for twenty days a month and meditate for a half hour a day.

60. I was invited to a Boston Ching Hai center. However, I was not allowed to either watch the meditation or see the videos of Ching Hai's teachings that are typically played as part of these sessions. I was, however, invited to share in the excellent Vietnamese food served afterward and participate in light discussion. Given such impediments to fieldwork, my comments will be confined to publicly available DVDs the organization produced from two retreats. While the DVDs were limited productions of only question-and-answer sessions held between participants and Ching Hai, they are still a rich record of her interactions and ideas.

61. Journalists, even those with no background in Religious Studies, seem to have a very negative visceral reaction to either Ching Hai or her organization. The Rick Ross Institute has links to approximately twenty articles criticizing Ching Hai either for her crass materialism, environmental degradation, religious synthesis, or personality cult. http://www.rickross.com/groups/suma_ching.html (accessed May 13, 2011).

62. In *The Key to Immediate Enlightenment,* Ching Hai expressed the following: "Always having male masters is boring. We need a change. You know, being a female spiritual teacher has also some advantages. Like, many women do not like, or feel shy, talking to men teachers, so maybe they find it easier to communicate with a female teacher." Supreme Master Ching Hai. 2001. *The Key to Immediate Enlightenment,* Taipei: Supreme Master Ching Hai International Association Publishing Co., Ltd., p. 166.

63. *The Key to Immediate Enlightenment,* p. 206.

CROSSCURRENTS

HINDUISM WITHOUT RELIGION
Amma's Movement in America

Amanda J. Huffer

As Hindu new religious movements globalize and disseminate their theological messages outside of India, they have a substantive tendency to wrestle with the category of the "Hindu" in their rhetoric and practices. While diasporic temple communities of ethnically Indian immigrants frequently embrace a Hindu identity as a means to take their place "at the multicultural table,"[1] transnational gurus and modern practitioners of yoga both have a unique legacy of tension with the category of the "Hindu." Some disavow the category entirely claiming the terms "spiritual" and "spirituality" as more effective markers and distance themselves from the perceived orthodoxies of Hindu religiosity by using a decontextualized theolinguistic register to signify more egalitarian, democratic, inclusive, ecumenical, and universalistic impulses. Very few of these types of modern global movements that derive their roots, practices, and theologies from Hindu religiosity proudly proclaim themselves to be Hindu. But why?

For many, the active distancing from the Hindu religiosity of their roots develops in tandem with their rise to global fame. As Tulasi Srinivas tells us, "No longer rooted in traditional Hinduism, the new sacred person of Sai Baba is disembedded from the religiocultural milieu and is free to travel across the global network."[2] But do global guru movements perceive this distancing from "traditional Hinduism" as a necessary correlation to becoming globally marketable? Does this signify that Western audiences (and even modern Indian ones) are unprepared to accept Hinduism with its plurality of particular and localized formations and even suggest a continued prejudice against Hindus and Hinduism as many staunch Hindu advocates would have us believe? Or has the historical legacy of the extraction of a generalized ecumenical universalism, often based in derivative forms of Advaita Vedantic philosophy, become so ingrained that it constitutes an independent religious category, nearly complete in its dissociation from its broader religious context of Hinduism?

Turning our gaze toward the pragmatic, one might argue that this ambivalence toward the category of the "Hindu" stems from discomfort with the fact that the term "Hindu" can readily be defined as a religio-ethnic category and one bound to a particular sacred geography: India. Thus, when attempting to reach geographically exogenous non-Indian Hindu audiences, [Hindu] gurus must at least deal with the potential for, if not the prior existence of, categorical dissonance among their followers. They must preempt the possibility that potential non-Indian Hindu recruits will question, "How can I follow this [Hindu] guru, if Hindu religiosity is a religio-cultural birthright available only to ethnically Indian Hindus?"

Or to speak in the stark terms of materialism, it might simply be the fact that the language of spirituality sells more effectively to global audiences, among both practitioners who identify with non-Hindu religious denominations and by the increasing populations of those who have become disillusioned by mainline Christian traditions.

The active distancing of largely Hindu ideologies, practices, discourses, and so on from the category of Hindu religion engenders the often virulent contemporary debates in which Indian Hindu activists attempt to reclaim contemporary modalities (such as yoga) as Hindu, while many of their practitioners staunchly defend their spiritual (non-Hindu) foundations (Vitello 2010). Recently, the head of the Hindu American Foundation touched on the commonplace marketing of Hinduism as spirituality, when he explained, "our issue is that yoga has thrived, but Hinduism has lost control of the brand."[3] Like yoga, Advaita Vedantic theology has been branded globally as "spirituality" by religious leaders who locate their roots in India and draw heavily from Hindu religiosity. But also like yoga, this particular strain of Hindu theology, often termed neo-Vedanta, has been adapted and transformed, sometimes to the point of non-recognition in order to make it palatable to diverse (both intra-Hindu and inter-religious) audiences. The rhetorical history of transnational gurus in the West shows us that the majority of them have chosen to implement generalized universalistic principles usually derived from Advaita Vedanta and couched in the language of spirituality, but dissociated from the greater context of Hinduism in order to garner popular acceptance of their "foreign" religiosity.

Regardless of the multiplicity of motivations behind this disassociation from the category of the Hindu, there are serious and perhaps unexpected consequences. When modern proponents of Hindu-derived practices and theologies argue that their innovations are spiritual rather than religious, or more specifically, Hindu, they effectively relegate the category of the Hindu to that which is traditional, stagnant, ritualistic, and so on and in the process they siphon off its potential for innovation and renewal in modernity. This categorical distancing echoes that of many of the participants in new [Hindu] religious movements, who also seek to detach themselves from "traditional" Hindu religiosity, believing it to be a signifier of backwards, ritualistic, hierarchical, and anti-modern sensibilities. In so doing, both parties stymie the process of Hindu religiosity's adaptations to "multiple modernities" (Appadurai 1996, Eisenstadt 2000, Tambiah 2000), which ultimately results in the antiquation and fixity of our understanding of what it means to be Hindu. This active process of siphoning results in the fact that youth searching for a Hindu identity are more often than not restricted to conservative and orthodox options because the innovative and liberalistic options have been recoded as spirituality. Thus, we might imagine that the language of spirituality may unwittingly contribute to the active rise in Hindutva ideologies, which are of particular concern in diaspora contexts where the desire to represent an authentically Hindu identity is palpable.

Scholars, for their part, have largely reflected this distinction rather than challenging it. In attempting to describe and define the products of this disassociation from "traditional" Hinduism, they somewhat uncomfortably innovate new terminologies to evocate the Hindu-like activities of many avenues of global Hindu religiosity, e.g., Hindu-derived or Hindu spirituality (Huffer 2010, Sharma 2006). In his recent work, *American Veda*, Philip Goldberg differentiates the modernist form of "Vedanta-Yoga" as "India's leading export," while George D. Chryssides analyzes "Hindu NRMs [New Religious Movements]" and rightly notes the absence of "distinctively Indian village practices...that are less palatable to westerners."[4] Lola Williamson recently went so far as to champion an entirely new category of [Hindu] religiosity, developing the term Hindu-Inspired Meditation Movements (HIMM) to denote the dual influences of ethnic-Hindus and theologically kaleidoscopic non-Indian Hindu spiritual seekers who comprise devotee populations. She argues that HIMMs are a new religion consisting of the hybridized influences of Hindu religiosity and "Western traditions of individualism and rationalism."[5] Noting the dissimilarity to what we might precariously term "traditional" Hindu religiosity, some scholars have opted for the disavowal of the term "Hindu" entirely, instead locating contemporary [Hindu] hybridity within the realm of "Indic" religiosity (Srinivas 2010) or "modernist" approaches as opposed to Hindu "traditionalism" (Warrier 2006).

My endeavor here examines closely one influential contemporary transnational guru, Amritanandamayi Ma (also known as Amma, the Malayalam [and more generally South Indian] term for "Mother"), who, like many of her contemporaries, actively disavows the category of religion in favor of spirituality. In addressing the category of Hinduism, Amma exhibits an ambivalence, in which she simultaneously exalts Hinduism as the most tolerant and ecumenical of the world's religions but also attempts to transcend the categories of Hinduism and religion to promote a non-denominational spirituality. Amma creates her vision of spirituality by drawing on the universalistic monism of Advaita Vedantic [Hindu] discourses and offering an expansive interpretation of Hinduism. With regard to her systematized orthopraxy, she performs and subsidizes rituals, practices, and administrative hierarchies that are undeniably Hindu. I juxtapose Amma's discourses with ethnographic data from her devotees in order to question precisely what is at stake in her somewhat commonplace move to promote discourses of spirituality instead of Hindu religion in her global transnational guru movement.

On universalism

But how do we get from the language of Hindu "religion" to that of "spirituality"? Ironically, one of the most effective theological resources that many of these [Hindu] new religious movements employ to obfuscate the category of the Hindu stems from within Hindu religiosity itself, in the form of neo-Vedantic universalism. Contemporary gurus have popularized hallmark Vedic maxims of universalism and ecumenicalism, such as "*ekam sat vipraha bahudha vadanti*" or "Truth is one, the wise call it by many names" (*Ṛg Veda*, 1.164.46) and famous Upaniṣadic maxims, such as "*tat tvam asi*: Thou art That," or "*ayam atma brahma:* This Self is Brahman." These textual citations are used to evidence several fundamental claims: first, the essential unity of all living creatures and God (conceived as both immanent and transcendent), which one must realize by pulling aside the curtain of *māyā* (illusion); second, the realization of this ultimate reality is *mokṣa* (liberation) attained through personal development by means of spiritual practice and discipline, and third, the viability of a variety of means and methods to accessing that essential Truth.[6] Historically, the systematized philosophical school of Advaita Vedanta can be traced to Shankara's eighth-century commentary on the *Brahma Sūtras* (*Vedanta Sūtras*), but contemporary gurus often anachronistically attribute its roots to the Upaniṣads and the *Bhagavad Gītā*, both of which exhibit proto-Advaita Vedantic sensibilities. Many modern proponents, like Aiya, the temple priest/guru in Corinne Dempsey's ethnographic account of a goddess temple in upstate New York, explain neo-Vedantic sensibilities with the metaphor that like there are many rivers flowing into oceans with a variety of names, still all of these ultimately converge in the same body of water; so too is the nature of the world's religions eventually leading to one Ultimate Truth.[7] This modernist interpretation of Advaita Vedanta provides the foundation for a universalistic idiom that subsumes the multiplicity of difference into a singular conception of cosmic unity. It also resonates among Americans, many of whom easily elide it with Unitarianism, pantheism, and the traces of New Thought and Theosophy that continue to exert their influence in what Catherine Albanese terms American "metaphysical religion."[8]

Universalizing discourses present general normative claims that aim to speak to and represent all of humanity while camouflaging the fact that they are extracted from particular and particularizing ideologies. Characterized by the obfuscation of difference and particularity, universalizing discourses exert systemic violence upon differences between a multiplicity of religious expressions, which is often overlooked in favor of their unifying tendencies. The European universalisms of Enlightenment reason and rationality fueled the colonial endeavors of empire building directed at asserting Western hegemony across the globe. Proponents of Islamic universalism attempt to construct a pan-Islamic *ummah* that claims to represent and fulfill the social and religious needs of all of humanity. Hindu universalisms, in turn, also derive from the obfuscation of real differences between religious sects, people, and cultures. In their claims to universality, proponents not only minimize the importance of the particularities of subjects' self-identities, but they claim to represent those particularities by supplanting them with generalizing principles. In each of these cultural traditions, universality becomes a criterion and a site of conflict of who (and which universalist ideology) is best equipped to represent humanity. Thus, as Étienne Balibar suggests, in speaking of universalism, we instead must speak of multiple universalisms and recognize these claims as contested spaces constructed by political motivations.[9]

By focusing their attentions on universalisms, such as "One God/many paths," it might appear that contemporary gurus aim to parallel explicitly the universalisms of the Christian tradition, perhaps supposing that these maxims will ring familiar for Western audiences outside of India, many of whom have relations to Christian traditions. In these pithy maxims, they may find echoes of the Pauline demonstration of "the subsumption of the Other by the Same...how a universal thought, proceeding on the basis of the worldly proliferation of alterities (the Jew, the Greek, women, men, slaves, free men, and so on) *produces* a Sameness and an Equality (there is no longer either Jew, or Greek, and so on)."[10] In Paul's preaching, differences and particularities exist in the world, but they are not granted the subjectivity of truth; they must be transcended through faith, hope, and love to reach God. In Alain Badiou's summation, "[T]hese fictitious beings, these opinions, customs, differences, are that to which universality is addressed; that toward which love is directed; finally, that which must be traversed in order for universality itself to be constructed, or for the genericity (*généricité*) of the true to be imminently deployed."[11] Similarly, in Advaita Vedantic universalism worldly alterities are imagined as fictitious; they are illusions (*māyā*) that must be recognized as such, dissolved into monism in order to recognize the ultimate sameness and equality of all phenomena. In the universalism of the Advaita Vedantic lens, there is only monism (*sarvo brahman*: everything is Brahman); the existence of actual difference (and hence multiplicity) itself is denied. To use categories often deployed to translate Indic philosophical concepts, *ultimate* difference is revealed to be only *conventional* difference. The non-dual monism of neo-Vedanta cannot accept a plurality of opinions, tastes, creeds, prophets, or Gods without undermining its own philosophical foundations.

Spiritual but not religious

Many contemporary gurus use the unifying language of spirituality because it enables them to speak in a language that resonates with disparate and diverse audiences. Their contemporary eclectic and disunified audiences demand a transidiomatic theolinguistic register that Srinivas Aravamudan terms "Guru English," a cosmopolitan method of communication that aims to appeal to populations (and audiences) stemming from a variety of religio-cultural backgrounds.[12] The transidiomatic theolinguistic register of Advaita Vedantic philosophy enables culturally embedded spokespeople to transgress the particularities of Hindu religiosity in order to speak to global audiences in terms of generalized ethics, morality, and humanism. It is a product of the cultural encounter between India and the "West," which aims to translate and evangelize Hindu ideology by cloaking its particularities in universalistic rhetoric. It is perhaps no surprise then that the upswell of this new brand of neo-Vedantic universalism marks its beginnings at the fomenting moments of the Hindu Renaissance of the eighteenth and nineteenth centuries and similarly emerges from the cultural apologetics of the elite (largely Bengali) literati within the dialectical legacies of colonialism and orientalism.

This type of register is also vital for devotees, many of whom find the generalist and unifying language of spirituality to be an effective tonic of similitude as globalization has rapidly increased the abutment of radical differences through cultural diffusion, intercultural encounters, and a cosmopolitan panoply in the marketplace of religious ideas. Additionally, it also appeals to those who have disassociated from the particularities of a sectarian religious tradition and seek eclectic and alternative religiosities based in the unmediated pursuit of personal experiences of the supernatural. In fact, while spirituality is a notoriously nebulous term to define, there is something definitive within its focus on unmediated and internal experience of transcendence dissociated from any particular form of divinity, which distinguishes it from the category of religion. Robert Wuthnow defines spirituality as "a state of being related to a divine, supernatural, or transcendent order of reality or, alternatively, as a sense or awareness of a suprareality that goes beyond life as ordinarily experienced."[13] Martin Riesebrodt rightly notes that "the now widespread notion of 'spirituality' continues the individualistic orientation of Romantic discourse."[14] In fact, the modern definition of *spirituality* closely resembles the romanticism inherent in the highly interior and ecumenical terms with which William James famously defined *religion* as "the feelings, acts, and experiences of individual men in their solitude, so far as they apprehend themselves to stand in relation to whatever they may consider the divine."[15] Thus, the modern discourses of spirituality direct us toward the internal rather than the external and the experiential rather than the institutional; the term spirituality signifies the individual's personalized quest for an unmediated experience of the transcendent.

In the United States, the accelerating trend toward supplanting Christian church membership with self-defined alternative and eclectic spiritualities has supplemented the entrée of the new religious category "spiritual but not religious" (SBNR), which, as Philip Goldberg argues, has developed an entire discursive register, a *"lingua spiritus"* among those who hybridize and adapt Asian religions for Western audiences and their followers.[16] In fact, in surveys conducted between 1999 and 2002 in the United States, persons claiming this categorical status ranged from 16 to 39 percent of the American population.[17] Many who replace the term *religion* with *spirituality* aim to avoid the negative valences of that which is often associated with religion. As Robert C. Fuller tells us, "The word *spiritual* gradually became associated with the private realm of thought and experience while the word *religious* came to be connected with the public realm of membership in religious institutions, participation in formal rituals, and adherence to official denominational doctrines."[18] This increased emphasis on the privatization of religion reconfigured as spirituality (and the corresponding promotion of personal spiritual experience) might be read productively as a pragmatic sociocultural remedy to the potential for conflict and divisiveness. Many see this move as the inevitable consequence of the direct proximity and immediate accessibility of multiple religions interacting in the public sphere augmented by the increased mobility inherent to globalization (Luckmann 1967, Bellah 1985, Wuthnow 2003).

Similarly, contemporary Hindu religious spokespersons relate the term religion to a bounded set of doctrines substantiated by authorities and institutions who assert their exclusivist worldviews. In their views, the term religion emphasizes obligatory ritual actions to appease a transcendent God, whereas the term spirituality notions toward the inner transformation of the individual in order to foment the recognition of the imminent God within. Many of these spokespersons' ideological lineages can be traced to the neo-Vedantic universalisms of the eighteenth-century religious reformer Rammohan Roy and his Hindu-Unitarian society of the Brahmo Samaj. In 1893, at the World's Parliament of Religions in Chicago, Pratap Chandra Mazumdar, representing the Brahmo Samaj, similarly attached importance to "faith," "intuition," and "spiritual" experiences as opposed to doctrinal "religion." Speaking of the mission of the Brahmo Samaj, he explained, "It [Dogmatism] is the lifeless mass of complex theology, inherited by tradition, enforced by external authority, unrealized by spiritual experience, contradicted repeatedly by the spirit of the times and the ascertained laws of things, that the Brahma Samāj repudiates…The great and really profound doctrines of religion are…deposited within the mind in imperceptible accretions by the deep flow of spiritual impulses."[19] He envisioned a spiritual life as one comprised of intimate experiences of transcendence cultivated with the aid of devotions to and guidance from prophets. Mazumdar's dichotomy between dogma and spiritual experience created a Hindu-derived prototype for the contemporary distinction between religion and spirituality.

The ecumenical and universalistic neo-Vedantic ideas of the Brahmo Samaj, which fascinated American Unitarians as early as Rammohan Roy's articles in the *Christian Register*, profoundly influenced the tendency of contemporary transnational gurus to supplant Hindu religiosity with Advaita Vedantic universalistic spirituality. Swami Vivekananda (and many of his contemporaries and subsequent gurus) made "a conscious decision to emphasize a universal, adaptable Vedanta-Yoga, and to keep aspects of Hinduism that might be construed as cultist or idolatrous in the background, as a family might put exotic décor in a closet when conservative guests come over."[20] Nearly thirty years later, Paramahansa Yogananda (founder of the Self-Realization Fellowship) also argued that, "If by religion we understand only practices, particular tenets, dogmas, customs, and conventions, then there may be grounds for the existence of so many religions. But if religion means primarily God-consciousness, or the realization of God both within and without, and secondarily a body of beliefs, tenets, and dogmas, then, strictly speaking, there is but one religion in the world, for there is but one God."[21]

In distancing themselves from the perceived orthodoxies and ritualism of Hindu religiosity, many contemporary proponents express their spirituality through the (also Hindu) ideal of *sanatana dharma* (or the eternal truth/law). They use the term *sanatana dharma* to dissociate from the business and potential sectarianism of the religious category of Hinduism. In this popular view, *sanatana dharma* is distinct because it is not an "*–ism*" at all. Proponents distance *sanatana dharma* from the business of religion by arguing that it is instead a way of being, a method, a system of values, focused on the personal experience of an immanent and transcendent God. Furthermore, one may accept *sanatana dharma* without altering one's prior allegiance to a particular religion or faith. This caveat proves particularly useful when appealing to both Hindu and non-Hindu global audiences. While Hindus may be linked together through sacred geography, ethnicity, ritual actions, and an inherited wealth of religious scriptures, modern followers of *sanatana dharma* need only ascribe to a "philosophy of life," which can coexist with a variety of religious beliefs and practices.

Amma's movement uses this categorical distinction to advocate a form of religious tolerance in which devotees are encouraged to maintain their extant religious worldviews but also fold themselves into Amma's religiosity. Amma often highlights the parallels between the various world religions, from which she concludes, "though expressed in different ways, the principle conveyed here is the same. The import of all these sayings is that: As the same Soul, or Atman, abides in all things, we must see and serve all as One. It is the people's distorted intellect that makes them interpret these principles in a limited way."[22] Amma's interpretation attempts to minimize differences and highlight similarities among world religions, but ultimately she reads each religion through the lens of Advaita Vedantic monism: "we must see and serve all as One."

Beneath this ecumenical surface, one finds that *sanatana dharma* is in actuality a recoding of Hinduism, for example, Amma says, "The great souls living in different countries during different epochs gave their disciples instructions on how to attain God (or the Ultimate Truth). These instructions later became different religions. But that which in India became Sanatana Dharma consists of the everlasting principles, values, and ethical teachings that were revealed to a large number of Self-realized souls as their own experience. [sic] Later it came to be known as Hinduism. It is all encompassing."[23] In this explanation, *sanatana dharma* is not only proto-Hinduism, but it is also the wellspring for all world religions. When intertwined with a nationalistic zeal, *sanatana dharma* becomes the underlying spiritual essence of all religions and India, the sacred geography of its genesis, becomes guru to the world. As Amma says, "Every place has a heart center...In the same way, India is the heart center of the world. Sanatana Dharma, which originated here in India, is the source of all other paths. When the very word 'Bharatam' [India] is heard, we experience the pulse of peace, beauty and light. The reason is that Bharat is the land of the mahatmas. It is the mahatmas who transmit the life force not only to India, but to the whole world."[24] *Sanatana dharma* is proto-Hinduism without the baggage of religion, imagined as transcendent, eternal, value and ethics based, ecumenical, and above all based in the internal experiences of individuals. Much like the inclusivism of liberal Protestants, to which it is often a respondent, this type of rhetoric becomes a similarly inclusivistic theology, a topic to which I will return shortly.

The ideology of the eternal, unchanging *sanatana dharma* combines with neo-Vedantic monism and as such subsumes difference into a metacategory that coincides with one particular Hindu sectarian ideology. In it there is no space for or acceptance of the cultural encounter of radical difference; in fact, it is the very substance of multiculturalism—difference—that is undermined. The universalistic monism of neo-Vedantic philosophy, while often articulated in service of multiculturalism, interfaith dialogue, and ecumenism, is in actuality its antithesis. For example, like Yogananda cited previously, Amma denies the actuality of diversity among world religions when she asserts that there is only one omnipresent omnipotent God, whom various religions envision in different forms. She says,

> Gods? There are not many gods. There is only one God. The different forms are only to enable people to adopt and use the form

which they like, according to their mental tendencies. In this way the goal is attained easily. People in different countries call Him by different names. God is not many because of that...The same girl is looked upon as a sister by her brother and as a wife by her husband. The younger brother sees her as his eldest sister. There is no change in the person; she is the same girl. In a similar way, the Power is one but the names differ.[25]

Herein lies the commonly heard neo-Vedantic solution to the variety of deities in the Hindu pantheon, first implemented widely in the modern period as a response to colonial and orientalist critiques of Hindu polytheism. But instead of smoothing over differences between Hindu Shaivites, Shaktas and Vaishnavas, here the suppression of religio-cultural differences takes on a globalized scale interlocuting between "world religions."

It is this interlocutive impulse between world religions that substantiates the displacement of the category of religion in favor of a universalistic spirituality. It has at its heart the pragmatic goal of uniting diverse (and often conflicting) ideologies. In her discourses, Amma often places the blame for wars and social injustices at the feet of religion and religious divisiveness. Speaking to the United Nations General Assembly in 2000, Amma said, "The very words 'nation' and 'religion' tend to connote division and diversity."[26] Whereas "true religion" is spirituality, a spirituality that recognizes that "there is one Truth that shines through all of creation"[27] In one of her most commonly employed illustrations, she explains that "religion" is the husk, while "spirituality" is the "kernel." In other words, we must shuck the external properties of religion, which prevent us from enjoying its essence, spirituality. She says, "Instead of focusing on the essence of the religious principles of love and compassion, we focus on the external rituals and traditions, which vary from religion to religion. That is how these religions, which were originally meant to foster peace and a sense of unity among us, became instrumental in spreading war and conflict. If we are willing to abide by the essential principles of religions, without being overly concerned about their external features and superficial aspects, religion will become a pathway for world peace."[28] Thus, she maintains that we must transfer emphasis from religions (plural) to spirituality (singular) in order to foster an environment that minimizes religious conflict and promotes intercultural unity. She accentuates what she believes to be the core religious values of love and compassion in order to argue for a spiritual global ethic, freed from the sectarianism and differences in orthopraxy which divide humanity into various religious allegiances. Pragmatically, Amma sees this shift in focus as a necessary component to universal peace and prosperity among the diverse populations of the world's religions.

However, in this case as well, her framing of the essence of religion as spirituality cannot be dislocated from the context from which she derives her inspiration: Hindu religiosity. Amma says that she is promoting universalistic principles that transcend any particular religion, when in fact she is espousing a paradigmatically Hindu philosophy, championed as universal. She says, "My children, according to Hinduism, there is Divinity in everything; everything is an embodiment of God. Humans and God are not two; they are one. Divinity lies latent in every human being. Hinduism teaches that anyone can realize the Divinity within through self effort. The Creator and creation are not separate. The Creator (God) manifests as creation. In Hinduism, to realize this non-dual truth is considered to be the ultimate goal of life."[29] In this way, like her predecessors of the Hindu Renaissance and many of her contemporaries, Amma transforms the Advaita Vedantic strain of Hindu religiosity into the hallmark philosophy of Hinduism. In so doing, she propagates and reinforces the contemporary depiction of Hinduism (in its entirety) as Advaita Vedantic monism, a (mis)representation that is particularly ubiquitous in global arenas. Amma, like many other modern transnational gurus, extracts this transidiomatic theolinguistic register of universalism—exemplified through the language of spirituality—for its ease of transference and its ability to resonate with diverse audiences. She deploys Advaita Vedantic universalism alternately in the reductionistic modality as representative of the whole of Hinduism or in the disassociative modality as entirely unaffiliated with Hinduism in favor of a tenuous assertion of its roots in non-denominational spirituality.

Ecumenism and tolerance

In either case, gurus espousing the universalistic monism of Advaita Vedantic theology under the rubric of spirituality often accompany it with claims to its ecumenism and tolerance toward other religious worldviews. While modern gurus often promote ecumenism and tolerance as universalistic ideals, it does not take much probing beneath the surface to find their underlying belief that ecumenism and tolerance are, in fact, the hallmarks of a distinctively Hindu brand of spirituality. It is this ambivalence toward the category of the Hindu that reveals oscillating patterns of affiliation: non-Hindu (universalistic/spiritual) when proselytizing the particular theology of Advaita Vedanta and Hindu when appealing to often valorized humanistic ideals (ecumenism and tolerance). Are ecumenism and tolerance Hindu ideals as they are often marketed to be? Observing the religio-political advances of the Hindu right in the past thirty years, one might answer a vehement *no*. But careful attention to the rhetoric of modern transnational gurus who derive their global followings through the implementation of a theolinguistic register of neo-Vedantic universalism might suggest a qualified *yes*.

Like many debates, perhaps a closer investigation into semantics, in this case those of the Hindu use of the term "tolerance," may direct us toward a more productive and perhaps even more definitive answer. The Hindu vision of religious tolerance is more aptly termed "inclusivism," meaning that it validates and includes theologies and prophets from other religions. Peter van der Veer effectively argues that the Hindu conception of religious tolerance is a product of "a specific orientalist history of ideas." It is an Enlightenment discourse derived from "an abstraction and universalization of religion that is part of the Western discourse of 'modernity.'" As a doctrinal notion religious tolerance has "no specific place in Hindu discursive traditions," but it was readily incorporated so that "it has come to dominate Hindu discourse on Hinduism, to the point where tolerance is now viewed as one of the most important characteristics of Hinduism."[30]

Hindus not only *tolerate* other religiosities, but they incorporate them through its theological system of what Paul Hacker terms "hierarchical relativism."[31] This formulation depends on the theological opinion that avatars (bodily manifestations) of the One true god who is formless (Brahman) operate in different ways with different purposes on a hierarchical scale of importance. In van der Veer's language, "The general idea seems to be that the other paths do not have to be denied as heretical but that they are inferior and thus cater to inferior beings."[32] We can see this tendency in a multiplicity of textual and practical examples within the complexities of sectarian relations among various types of Hindus (from Shiva portrayed as a *gopī* [a female devotee of Krishna] in the region of Braj, to Rama *bhakta* devotional sects subordinating Krishna to Rama). This same hierarchical relativism and inclusivism that characterizes the historical relations among Hindu sects also exemplifies the manner in which contemporary Hindus often relate to other religions. Much to the chagrin of Christian missionaries in India, Hindus demonstrate a willingness to incorporate the prophets and deities of other religions into the Hindu pantheon. Additionally, Hindus have a legacy of incorporating extra-Hindu ideas into their extensive theological corpus often demonstrating parallel themes already endemic to the scriptures of the Hindu traditions. With a tradition as diverse and multifarious as Hinduism, it is relatively easy to find nearly any theological or secular ideology somewhere in its voluminous textual history.

With regard to the contemporary Hindu claims to be the theological birthplace of religious tolerance and ecumenism, many proponents again use the concept of *sanatana dharma* in order to promote an inclusivistic stance. Amma iterates a common assertion in saying, "Hinduism isn't against anyone. Nor does it require anyone to give up his or her religion or faith. In fact, it considers it an unrighteous act to destroy someone's faith. According to Sanatana Dharma, all religions are different pathways to the same goal. It doesn't negate anything. Everything is included. For a Hindu there is no such thing as a separate religion. Originally, such a concept didn't exist in India."[33] At the 1893 World's Parliament of Religions, Swami Vivekananda famously declared a similar interpretation, "I am proud to belong to a religion which has taught the world both tolerance and universal acceptance. We believe not only in universal toleration, but we accept all religions as true."[34]

A Hinduism without religion

Amma argues for both the universalistic monism of Advaita Vedanta (iterated as non-Hindu spirituality) *and* the presumed Hindu proclivity toward hierarchical relativism (iterated as ecumenism). In essence, she attempts simultaneously to both expand and transcend the category of Hinduism. She articulates a theological position which on the surface appears to be quite ecumenical and palatable to interfaith dialogues, to which she is often invited at the most prestigious levels.[35] Because she presents her worldview as "spiritual" instead of "religious," she is often regarded as a particularly effective mediatrix between the often conflicting voices of various religious traditions. For example at the Interfaith Summit during *Amritavarsham50* in 2003, Shri. Bawa Jain, Secretary General of the World Council of Religions addressed Amma directly and said, "It is Your mission and responsibility to unite the religious leaders of the world together in harmony and peace. You are not bound by religious institutions or traditions."[36] Many of her audiences, followers, and most ardent devotees also believe that in adhering to her message, they are being "spiritual, but not religious" and that their theology exists outside the boundaries of the religion of Hinduism when in fact, the very philosophical foundations that enable them to make that self-assessment derive from within Hinduism. The Advaita Vedantic monism with which they defend their ecumenism, universalism, and religio-cultural relativism signifies Shankara's hallmark contribution to Hindu theology.

Again, even when employing the discourse of spirituality as opposed to religion, Hindu roots are not far below the surface. Amma says, "India's culture is spirituality. The origin of spirituality, though it is beginningless, to speak in empirical terms, is the *Vedas*. Therefore, to preserve, protect and spread the *Vedic dharma* is equal to preserving, protecting and spreading the moral and spiritual values of the country which will help to uplift and unify its people. This alone will protect the country from a great down-fall."[37] Herein, the thin veneer of ecumenical spirituality shows its roots to be in the Vedas, the foundational scriptures for much of contemporary Hindu religiosity (in name if not always in practice). Amma's statement, laced with somewhat uncharacteristic Hindu nationalistic overtones [India = Vedic "spirituality"], reveals that even her idea of spirituality (as opposed to religion) must be understood as culturally embedded within a specifically Hindu cultural and discursive heritage, despite its pretense toward universality.

Many devotees wholeheartedly imbibe this categorical distancing between their spiritual worldviews and the perceived entrapments of religion and more particularly of Hinduism. They envision Amma as one who has Hindu roots, but transcends Hinduism and religion in general. One senior *brahmacāri* (renunciate aspirant), who lives at her ashram headquarters in India explained, "*She [Amma] transcends the religion, the*

Hindu religion as such. And personally I believe she is the best example of Hinduism—because it is an all-encompassing religion. It welcomes everybody there. It does not say that this is the right path for you or this is the only path for you. You can worship God or not worship God, worship God in any form, name, or formless. This is total freedom. This is what Amma does. You can worship Christ and be spiritual; you can worship Rama and be spiritual. Amma exemplifies the Hindu tradition to the max. *She transcends Hinduism, she is not religious; but she represents Hinduism, the best of Hinduism.* There is nothing religious about it, merely spiritual."[38] Notice how he defines Amma's discursive position toward Hinduism quite accurately, explaining that she simultaneously transcends and exemplifies/represents Hinduism. There is also significance in his concluding value judgment that the "best of Hinduism" is what is spiritual, while by contrast that which is not the "best of Hinduism" must be religious. A middle-aged Euro-American Amma devotee who developed her own eclectic spirituality while living in San Francisco, the American heartland of spiritual enterprise and exploration, explained, "Religion for me is static and narrow and dogmatic...But when we get into the spiritual life and the spiritual way of living, what we call spiritual—and it's really scientific, it's really scientific—then, when we can merge ourselves and our heart with science then that will be the final [stage]."[39] A Syrian-American self-defined "liberal Muslim" and Amma devotee iterated foundationally Advaita Vedantic principles to me when he explained that, "Truth is truth, God is God, and it is expressed in different forms vis-à-vis different traditions."[40]

In supplanting religion with spirituality, Amma creates a theology that resonates with many Hindus who ascribe to neo-Vedantic theology while simultaneously appealing to the inclusive perennialist ideologies of the variety of movements often characterized as "New Age" or "metaphysical religion" in the United States. Many of these argue that "we are all essentially one; all religions point to the same truth; the globe is a whole; unity prevails within diversity."[41] The complex cultural encounter between proponents of neo-Vedantic theology and metaphysical religions in the United States not only fuels these culturally adaptive discourses but also supports practical commonalities among populations of Indian Hindu and American spiritualist devotees who interact in many contemporary transnational guru movements.

In Amma's branding statements directed at reaching these transnational populations of potential devotees, she often translates her references to Hindu scriptures and Hindu orthopraxy into more culturally ambiguous and generalized terminology. One of the primary maxims that Amma uses, "Love and Serve" condenses her complex religious philosophy into two simple ideas, notably two ideas that make no definitive reference to her Hindu roots. Nor does her primary identity statement "Embracing The World" (branded Summer 2009) make any reference to her Hindu roots. Instead, Amma's organization increasingly endeavors to depict her as a global spiritual teacher with a dedication to healing suffering and contributing to humanitarian causes around the world.

One might conclude then that Amma and her organization have truly globalized and with so many of her discourses emphasizing the universal and spiritual aspects of religion, even to the point of "transcending" religion, that she has expanded beyond her religious roots that locate her within the Hindu traditions. However, that is not the case. In fact, it is quite the opposite. Amma's organization instantiates classically Hindu religious ideas, scriptural references, devotional music, and ritual practices as a matter of routine. Functionally speaking, it supports a commonplace Hindu administrative structure of *swamī-s, brahmachāri/ṇī-s,* and *sevā-ites* (hierarchically stratified in descending layers of religious authority) as well as multiple geographic centers in her ashrams and local *satsangs* (congregational gatherings).[42] It also routinely incorporates the full range of traditional Hindu rituals such as *darshan, pada puja, āratī, homas,* and special *pujas* and *yajñas*. In addition, Amma's movement encourages devotees to progress spiritually through daily mantra recitation, in-home *puja* ceremonies, and by practicing Amma's patented meditation technique, Integrated Amrita Meditation (IAM). Local *satsangs* and ashram communities congeal the devotional community and revivify Amma's presence by sponsoring rituals on special occasions that coincide with traditional Hindu festivals and religious celebrations; many also sponsor weekend meditation and yoga retreats, public discourses, *saṅkīrtan* (collective *bhajan* singing), and *sevā* (selfless service) projects.

Contemporary transnational guru movements of the present, thanks to a long legacy of predecessors who broke down cultural barriers, are largely free to express their particular religiosities without consternation from the general public. While there are certainly scandals (some more warranted than others), contemporary gurus in the United States "have fewer doors to break down, and they no longer attract overheated media coverage and trigger extremes of rapture and hostility."[43] While guru communities are still occasionally viewed askance among the general American populace, the ideas of karma yoga, hatha yoga, bhakti devotionalism, and ashram retreats have become integrated into the kaleidoscopic lens of popular American alternative religiosities. But although multiculturalism and the appreciation of diversity have largely triumphed over the assimilationist paradigms which have been predominant throughout the majority of American history, still [Hindu] gurus from India have hardly changed their theologies to reflect these developments. They continue to implement the "spiritual" universalistic ecumenism of Advaita Vedanta and tuck the particularities of its Hindu religious context in the closet (especially when speaking to diverse public audiences), much like their historical predecessors.

In essence, Swami Vivekananda spoke with as of yet unchallenged authority when he created the hierarchy between the "high spiritual flights of the Vedanta philosophy" and "the low ideas of idolatry with its multifarious mythology," which he presented to excited audiences at the 1893 World's Parliament of Religions and later to packed lecture halls across the United States. As Aravamudan notes, "The orientalists' broad delineation and separation of philosophical doctrine from popular religion—highbrow texts from lowbrow culture—is an early version of modern Hinduism already at work."[44] Here, Aravamudan points us to a key component of this puzzle: the distinction between "progressive" spirituality and "backwards" Hindu religion reifies orientalist conceptions of cultural and religious hierarchies.

That said, the orthopraxies, if not the rhetoric of contemporary gurus is changing. While still espousing the transidiomatic theolinguistic register of Advaita Vedanta, many contemporary transnational gurus have created cottage industries by offering services in particular devotional rituals, life-cycle ritual ceremonies, Vedic sacrifices (*yajñas* and *homas*), and so on. Amma's movement, in particular, demonstrates the discordant juxtaposition between universalistic "SBNR" rhetoric derived from Advaita Vedantic sources (often espoused to audiences who are unaware of its extraction from a Hindu context) and classically Hindu ritual practices. The popular ritualism of the movement signifies the shift in the multiculturalist American public's validation of difference, while its generalized rhetoric provides a blanket of security for those still uncomfortable with the influx of "foreign" religions.

In the cultural encounter between East and West, historically gurus adapted both their religious products and their rhetoric to non-Hindu audiences. Today, the product remains to some degree intact, while the rhetoric continues to adapt in order to allay fears and assuage the cultural translation. The contemporary attachment to the language of spirituality, an example of the transidiomatic theolinguistic register of neo-Vedantic universalism, signifies not the ecumenical interfaith dialogue that it often attempts to endeavor, but rather the lingering effects of the discomfort with cultural difference. Its nearly ubiquitous proliferation among transnational [Hindu] gurus is ample evidence that our multicultural aspirations have not yet reached fruition as to the acceptance of others, not as essentially the same, but as fundamentally different.

Conclusion

At the outset, I asked not only how, but why contemporary transnational gurus distance themselves from the category of religion and, in particular, that of Hinduism. In addressing the why, thus far I have argued primarily that gurus use the language spirituality in order to reach diverse populations and to resonate with Christocentric populations in particular (many of whom have become disillusioned with mainline Christianity). I have also suggested that gurus employ the non-denominational language of spirituality in order to stymie the potential for religio-cultural conflict in our rapidly globalizing world. Additionally, I would offer two hypotheses that may warrant further consideration: first, that these maxims reflect tendencies inherent to multiculturalism in the United States, and second, that gurus continue to perceive these cultural translations to be necessary in order to garner favor with American audiences.

Multiculturalism in the United States suggests that cultural communities be allowed and even encouraged to promote their particular ethnic heritage, so long as it does not overtly clash with the overarching commitment to proclaimed American values, such as liberty, democracy, and freedom. But often this "heritage, or 'culture' is not treated as a living set of social relations but as a timeless trait," evidencing an orientalist understanding of the static Other in contrast to the imagined dynamism of European cultures.[45] Vijay Prashad rightly argues that this understanding of the cultures of ethnic groups in the United States as static undergirds a fundamental discomfort with the ambiguities of difference and similarity. "Either people are all the same, or they are fundamentally different. There is little patience with the strategy that though people share much they are also dissimilar."[46] Recognizing this uncomfortable ambiguity, contemporary gurus venture toward the theolinguistics of the similarity (or even sameness) in the essence of all religions, perhaps in fear that their overt recognition of sometimes oppositional differences would eliminate their capacities to unite and appeal to diverse populations (which would also diminish their audiences and subsequent revenues). In this sense, their contributions signify an expansion of the tendency to construct avenues of similitude in the complex territories of diversity, which is evident in practical applications of multiculturalism.

Contemporary transnational gurus may also fear that espousing particular and foreign theologies to American audiences might place their movements within the more dangerous category of religious zealots proclaiming radical differences—in contemporary parlance often subsumed under the reductionistic category of "cult," or worse yet, "terrorist."[47] In fact, we might view the contemporary trend to reconceptualize Hindu orthodoxies into the universalistic theolinguistic register of Advaita Vedanta (voiced as spirituality) as a method for Hindus in the American diaspora to distance themselves from the generalized anti-Islamic sentiment directed at Muslims. If Hindus alter their orthodoxies to present themselves as the epitome of tolerance and ecumenicalism, they may escape the fate of their Muslim brethren, who are often condemned in the American public eye for their "fundamentalist" and "orthodox" religiosities. While this explanation supposes that contemporary gurus engage in calculated market research and modify their messages to suit particular audiences, the astute marketing teams in many of these transnational corporations make it a plausible possibility. And if so, then it might suggest that Americans of today are perceived to be quite similar to our compatriot audiences at the 1893 World's Parliament of Religions, who were largely delighted to discover in Swami Vivekananda's discourses a universalistic, ecumenical, and tolerant version of neo-Vedantic "spirituality," but rigidly opposed to the "heathen religion" of Hinduism. If underlying orientalism and the intolerance of true cultural difference continue to demand the translation of much of Hindu religiosity into the language of spirituality, then I fear that we may unwittingly create the foundations for a fearsome form of religion that will call itself Hindu, a form that feels it must distinguish itself from the discourses of "spirituality" by claiming its authenticity through the defining characteristics of its presumed antitheses: fundamentalism, orthodoxy, and intolerance. And as so many young South Asian immigrants search for tools with which to represent an "authentic" Hindu identity, this may be a dire consequence indeed.

Works cited

Albanese, Catherine L., 2008, *A Republic of Mind and Spirit*, New Haven, CT: Yale University Press.

Amritanandamayi Ma, 2004, "Living in Harmony," An address at the Millennium World Peace Summit of Religious and Spiritual Leaders, The United Nations General Assembly, August 29, 2000, Amritapuri, Kerala: Mata Amritanandamayi Mission Trust.

Amritanandamayi Ma, 2006a, "Understanding and Collaboration Between Religions," Delivered upon Amma's acceptance of the Fourth Annual James Park Morton Interfaith Award, May 2, 2006, Amritapuri, Kerala: Mata Amritanandamayi Mission Trust.

Amritanandamayi Ma, 2006b, *The Eternal Truth*, Amritapuri, Kerala: Mata Amritanandamayi Mission Trust.

Amritaswarupananda, Swami, 1991a, *Awaken Children! Dialogues with Sri Sri Mata Amritanandamayi Ma*, Vol. II, San Ramon, CA: Mata Amritanandamayi Center.

Amritaswarupananda, Swami, 1991b, *Awaken Children! Dialogues with Sri Sri Mata Amritanandamayi Ma*, Vol. III, San Ramon, CA: Mata Amritanandamayi Center.

Anonymous, 1926, *Leaders of the Brahmo Samaj*, Madras: G. A. Natesan & Co. Publishers.

Appadurai, Arjun, 1996, *Modernity at Large*, Minneapolis: University of Minnesota Press.

Aravamudan, Srinivas, 2005, *Guru English*, Princeton, NJ: Princeton University Press.

Asad, Talal, 1993, *Genealogies of Religion*, Baltimore, MD: Johns Hopkins University Press.

Badiou, Alain, 2003, *Saint Paul: The Foundation of Universalism*, Ray Brassier, translator, Stanford, CA: Stanford University Press.

Balagangadhara, S. N., 1994, "The Heathen in His Blindness...", Leiden, UK: Brill.

Balibar, Étienne, 2002, *Politics and the Other Scene*, London: Verso.

Bellah, Robert, 1985, *Habits of the Heart*, Berkeley: University of California Press.

Chryssides, George D., 2001, *Exploring New Religions*, New York: Continuum.

Dempsey, Corinne, 2006, *The Goddess Lives in Upstate New York*, Oxford: Oxford University Press.

Dubuisson, Daniel, 2003, *The Western Construction of Religion*, Baltimore, MD: Johns Hopkins University Press.

Eisenstadt, S. N., 2000, "Multiple Modernities," *Daedalus* 129, pp. 1–29.

Fuller, Robert C., 2001, *Spiritual but Not Religious*, Oxford: Oxford University Press.

Goldberg, Phillip, 2010, *American Veda*, New York: Harmony Books.

Halbfass, Wilhelm, 1998, *India and Europe*, New York: State University of New York Press.

Heelas, Paul, 1996, *The New Age Movement*, Oxford: Wiley-Blackwell.

Huffer, Amanda, 2010, "Darshan in a Hotel Ballroom: Amritanandamayi Ma's (Amma's) Communities of Devotees in the United States," Ph.D. Dissertation, University of Chicago.

James, William, 1985, *The Varieties of Religious Experience*, New York: Penguin Classics.

Kurien, Prema A., 2007, *A Place at the Multicultural Table*, New Brunswick, NJ: Rutgers University Press.

Luckmann, Thomas, 1967, *The Invisible Religion*, New York: Macmillan Press.

Prashad, Vijay, 2000, *The Karma of Brown Folk*, Minneapolis: University of Minnesota Press.

Riesebrodt, Martin, 2010, *The Promise of Salvation*, Chicago: University of Chicago Press.

Sharma, Arvind, 2006, *A Guide to Hindu Spirituality*, Bloomington, IN: World Wisdom.

Srinivas, Tulasi, 2010, *Winged Faith*, New York: Columbia University Press.

Tambiah, S.J., 2000, "Transnational Movements, Diaspora, and Multiple Modernities," *Daedalus* 129, pp. 163–94.

van der Veer, Peter, 1996, *Religious Nationalism*, New York: Oxford University Press.

Vitello, Paul, 2010, "Hindu Group Stirs Debate in Fight for the Soul of Yoga," New York Times, November 27.

Vivekananda, Swami, 1893, "Response to Welcome," World's Parliament of Religions, September 11, 1893, Complete Works of Swami Vivekananda, Vol. I, available at http://www.ramakrishnavivekananda.info/vivekananda/volume_1/vol_1_frame.htm, accessed on January 3, 2011.

Warrier, Maya, 2006, "Modernity and Its Imbalances: Constructing Modern Selfhood in the Mata Amritanandamayi Mission," *Religion* 36, pp. 179–95.

Williamson, Lola, 2010, *Transcendent in America: Hindu-Inspired Meditation Movements as New Religion*, New York: New York University Press.

Wuthnow, Robert, 2003, "Spirituality and Spiritual Practice," *The Blackwell Companion to Sociology of Religion*, Richard K. Fenn, editor, Malden, MA: Blackwell Publishing, pp. 306–20.

Notes

1. See Kurien, *A Place at the Multicultural Table*.
2. Srinivas, 91.
3. See Vitello, "Hindu Group Stirs Debate in Fight for the Soul of Yoga."
4. Chryssides, 203.
5. Williamson, 4.
6. Philip Goldberg supplies a similar list of seven "core Vedantic principles that we in the West have adapted." Goldberg, 10-11.
7. Dempsey, 186.
8. See Albanese, *A Republic of Mind and Spirit*.
9. Balibar, 146-74.
10. Badiou, 109.
11. Ibid., 98.
12. See Aravamudan, *Guru English*.
13. Robert Wuthnow, "Spirituality and Spiritual Practice," *The Blackwell Companion to Sociology of Religion*, 307.
14. Riesebrodt, 3.
15. James, 31.
16. Goldberg, 344.
17. Ibid., 22.
18. Fuller, 5.
19. *Leaders of the Brahmo Samaj*, 160.
20. Goldberg, 80.
21. Yogananda's speech at the International Conference of Religious Liberals, Boston, MA (1920), cited in Goldberg, 113.
22. Sri Mata Amritanandamayi Devi, Understanding and Collaboration Between Religions," 22.
23. Amritanandamayi Ma, *The Eternal Truth*, 10.
24. Amma, Chief Executive of Dharma, *Immortal Bliss*, 1st Quarter 2004, San Ramon: Mata Amritanandamayi Ma Center, 27.
25. Swami Amritaswarupananda, *Awaken Children!* Vol. II, 184.
26. Amritanandamayi Ma, "Living in Harmony," 20.
27. Ibid., 23.
28. Ibid., 28.
29. Sri Mata Amritanandamayi Devi, *The Eternal Truth*, 5.
30. van der Veer, 66-7.
31. Cited in van der Veer, *Religious Nationalism*, 68, see also Halbfass, *India and Europe*, 403-18.
32. van der Veer, 68.

33. Here, Amma rightly alludes to the fact that the term "religion" is a superimposed Western construct that has no direct correlate in Indic thought or languages. This point has been raised and debated among many scholars (Asad 1993, Balagangadhara 1994, Dubuisson 2003). I would also like to express gratitude to Pankaj Jain for reminding me that this entire discourse oscillating between the terms "religion," "spirituality," and "Hinduism" suggests a struggle with the modern dilemma of mapping western categories onto Indic ones. For example, if it were to adhere to indigenous Indic paradigms, the discourse might focus on Sanskritic terms such as "*dharma*," "*saṃskṛti*," and "*ādhyātmika*." The fact that the terms of debate are instead "religion," "spirituality," and "Hinduism" suggests that neo-Hinduism draws its tools of identity construction from both Western and Indic sources and cannot be extricated from the development of modern Indian understandings of subjectivity which emerged in dialogue with colonial power structures. Amritanandamayi Ma, *The Eternal Truth*, 21.

34. Swami Vivekananda, "Response to Welcome," World's Parliament of Religions, September 11, 1893.

35. Amma has presented on collaboration between the world religions at the Parliament of World Religions (1993), at the Interfaith Celebration of the United Nations (1995), to the UN General Assembly at the Millennium World Peace Summit of Religious and Spiritual Leaders (2000), at the Interfaith Center of New York (2006) upon her acceptance of the Fourth Annual James Parks Morton Interfaith Award, and many others.

36. Far-Reaching, *Immortal Bliss*, 1st Quarter 2004, San Ramon: Mata Amritanandamayi Ma Center, 25.

37. Swami Amritaswarupananda, *Awaken Children!* Vol. III, 297.

38. Interview with Surya, San Ramon programs, June 6, 2008.

39. Ibid.

40. Interview with Iqbal, San Ramon programs, June 9, 2008.

41. Heelas, 219.

42. I use the notation "*sevā-ites*" to reflect the Sanskrit root of the term, however, within the movement these volunteers are referred to with the Sanskrit/English hybrid term "sevites."

43. Goldberg, 328.

44. Aravamudan, 32.

45. Prashad, 112.

46. Ibid.

47. Here we might understand ISKCON's troubled history of legal accusations and scandals in the United States to be a potential warning to Hindu new religious movements to the consequences of espousing particularistic theologies that demand a high level of commitment from American followers.

CROSSCURRENTS

NEGOTIATING RELIGIOUS AND NATIONAL IDENTITIES IN CONTEMPORARY INDONESIAN ISLAMIC EDUCATION

Florian Pohl

Indonesia's political transformation since the fall of Suharto's authoritarian New Order regime in May 1998 has been nothing short of remarkable. For the third time, general elections were held in July 2009 in which Indonesians elected the national and regional legislative assemblies and directly chose a president. Largely peaceful and supported by organizations from a wide ideological and religious spectrum, these elections measure as a great success in the country's ongoing democratization process. Recent surveys, moreover, show the general openness and moderate outlook of the Indonesian Muslim population on questions of democracy, civil rights, and interfaith tolerance (Esposito and Mogahed 2007, Mujani 2007).[1] This trend toward participatory politics, perhaps surprisingly to some, has coincided with a notable resurgence of Islamic identity among the majority Muslim population. Measured by such indicators of personal piety as belief in God and performance of the five daily prayers, Indonesian Muslims rank well ahead of their sisters and brothers in other Muslim-majority nations (Hassan 2007). Similarly, polling data suggest growing support for Islamic-based law among a strong majority of Indonesian Muslims (Pew Global Attitudes Project 2011).

The perceived tension between these two currents has raised the question of how compatible the formation of a democratic public and political sphere is with the persistent revival of Islamic identity among the majority Muslim population. Such concerns have been heightened by a growing number of inner- and inter-religious conflicts. The list of some of the most visible events includes the 2005 fatwa of the Indonesian Ulama Council (MUI) condemning pluralism, secularism, and liberalism (Gillespie 2007), the violent attacks by members of Muslim vigilante organizations such as the Islamic Defenders Front (FPI) on participants in a rally for religious freedom at Jakarta's National Monument in June 2008, and, since 2008, a string of attacks on Christian and Ahmadiyah places of worship, particularly in West Java (International Crisis Groups [ICG] 2010). Finally, the hotel bombings of July 2009 in Jakarta, which were reminiscent of attacks in Bali and Jakarta between 2002 and 2005, are the latest reminder of the threat militant Muslim groups pose to communal harmony and peace in Indonesia.

Building trust across ideological and communal boundaries and promoting a public discourse marked by civility and respect for the rights of others are particularly significant within a country that is as religiously diverse as Indonesia. In light of inter- and intra-religious tensions, the need arises for new frameworks that allow the accommodation of religious diversity in a context characterized by strong confessional identities and convictions. Increasingly, this need is impacting how educational systems engage issues of religious diversity, co-citizenship, tolerance, and mutual understanding in their schools and curricula. Whereas experiences of ethnic and religious conflict have led to interfaith-oriented models of religious education in some Muslim-majority countries, such more inclusive approaches to religious education still are the exception in Indonesia. The continued prevalence of confessional models, however, does not indicate a lack of concern among Indonesian Muslim educators for civic education, inclusive citizenship, and interfaith harmony. This article highlights important educational programs and approaches through which different Islamic institutions have responded to the pluralist-democratic transformation in the post-Suharto era. These developments, it will become clear, not only reflect broader social and political trends but also indicate the significant political role Indonesia's Islamic schools play in shaping the ongoing public discourse on Islam and multi-religious citizenship.

Islamic education and Muslim schools in Indonesia

Islamic education is a potent source of identity formation in Indonesia. Ever since the early decades of the republic, the study of religion has been legally required of all students. There are a wide variety of educational institutions, both public and private, where all of this takes place. The state's support for Islam and Islamic education, however, is not the result of an Islamic constitution. Although close to 90 percent of its populations profess Islam, Indonesia is not an Islamic state, nor is Islam the state's official religion. Rather, the country is built constitutionally on five principles known as the Pancasila, the first of which is *ketuhanan* or "belief in one God." This unique foundation of the Indonesian state has allowed for a multi-religious conceptualization of national identity that recognizes six traditions as official religions. These include Protestant, Catholic, Hindu, Buddhist, and, more recently, Confucian communities next to the Muslim majority. Although national unity is not premised on membership in a specific religious community, the Pancasila indicates the state's interest in religion as a means to strengthening national identity. In the educational sector, this interest in religion means that the state supports and oversees the teaching of Islam and other religious traditions in the national education system through the work of the Ministry of National Education and the Ministry of Religious Affairs in both public and private schools.

The general public schools (*sekolah*) are non-sectarian in Indonesia. As in many other Muslim-majority countries, religious education in these public schools is organized along confessional lines where it is typically given for two hours per week.[2] State support for Islam, however, extends beyond the inclusion of Islamic education in the curriculum of the *sekolah*-type schools. The state also maintains its own network of Islamic schools (madrasas) and numerous state Islamic colleges and universities. The majority of Islamic schools, however, are found in the private sector. Private Islamic schools are mostly of two kinds: pesantrens and madrasas. The pesantrens are Indonesia's traditional boarding schools in which students live and study under the guidance of a religious scholar or *kiai*. Their traditionalist orientation is expressed in the pesantrens' commitment to maintaining the canon of classical scholarship in the Islamic sciences (Dhofier 1999). By contrast and different from its namesake in the Middle East and South Asia, the Indonesian madrasa operates as a day school with a curriculum that is not so much characterized by an exclusive emphasis on the religious sciences but by a deliberate balance and integration of general and religious subjects.

Official government statistics for the school year 2007–2008 show that the majority of Indonesia's students are educated in the institutions of the public system. Private Islamic institutions, however, occupy a significant share within the national education system. The country's 39,500 madrasas, about 90 percent of which are private, enroll more than 13 percent of the country's 48 million students (Departemen Pendidikan Nasional 2008). The number of pesantrens is more difficult to assess because of the historically informal and independent nature of their organization, but estimates range from 10,000 (Azra *et al.* 2007) to more than 14,000 (ICG 2003). In many of these public and private networks and institutions, Muslim educators have revised their schools' curricula and created new educational programs in response to the political changes in the post-Suharto era.

Islamic educational responses to the political transformation in the post-Suharto era

Islamic education in the national curriculum for state primary and secondary schools

Indonesia's new education legislation (Law 20/2003) passed in June 2003 has reinscribed the confessional nature of religious instruction in the non-sectarian public schools. Although religious education had been part of the public school curriculum for several decades, the new legislation went beyond previous regulations by stipulating that all students must receive regular instruction in their own religious tradition from a teacher of the same faith. One of the driving forces behind this piece of legislation was the political pressure from Muslim groups who were fearful of proselytizing in private Christian schools that enroll larger numbers of Muslim students. Opposition, however, arose not only from Christian educational institutions, now forced to employ Muslim instructors, but also from major Muslim organizations such as the Muhammadiyah and Nahdlatul Ulama over concerns that the new law inappropriately addressed the need for civic-religious education and interfaith understanding. Attention to questions of tolerance and good interfaith relations, however, has not been completely absent from the new law. Legislative deliberations were framed by a revision of the national curriculum that emphasized competency-based models of education and sought to connect the teaching of individual religions with the promotion of tolerance and good interfaith relations (Raihani 2007). Although the new curriculum in religious education maintains the confessional orientation, notes Leirvik, "the latest revision of the curricula may point in the direction of a more unifying vision that stresses the civic dimension of religious education" (Leirvik 2004, p. 228).

The less optimistically inclined, however, will point out that the tolerance-promoting and harmony-building momentum of the new state curriculum remains severely limited by its narrow, constitutionally oriented conceptualization of religious pluralism and the lack of meaningful Islamic frameworks in which to advance new and accommodating perspectives on religious diversity. As Baidhawy points out, the new curriculum is encumbered by its continued reliance on the Pancasila's narrow notion of religious diversity that inadequately reflects Indonesia's rich religious diversity and sanctions a very limited notion of religious freedom (Baidhawy 2007, p. 18). What is more, although the curriculum asserts as a main objective that the study of Islam foster respect for followers of other religious traditions and that it contribute to the harmony between different religious communities and to the unity of the Indonesian nation, the concretization and translation of these aspirational goals into tangible teaching units in the curriculum remains underdeveloped. Finally, the dearth of explicit topics and materials is complicated by the absence of a theological framework in which basic ideas and principles of tolerance and pluralism could be discussed from within the Islamic tradition.

Civic education in the state system of Islamic higher education
Islamic theological frameworks for the development of thought and action on interfaith relations, pluralism, democracy, and human rights, which are largely absent from the curriculum for state primary and secondary schools, find explicit expression in the civic education program developed in the state system of Islamic higher education over the past decade. Its network currently includes thirty-three State Islamic Colleges (STAIN), thirteen State Islamic Institutes (IAIN), and six State Islamic

Universities (UIN) with campuses in almost all of the nation's provinces (Kementerian Agama Republik Indonesia 2008). The state system's leadership in citizenship education stands in continuity with a long history of intellectual openness and instructional innovation. The modernizing of Islamic higher education has included the continual upgrading of many IAINs into State Islamic Universities (UIN), which integrate Islamic sciences with disciplines in the general sciences such as chemistry, accounting, English language and literature, and medicine. Educational innovation has also aimed at the study of Islam itself through the introduction of non-dogmatic historical and contextual approaches (Azra *et al.* 2007, p. 189). Reacting to the changing socio-political demands on the education system after 1998, the state Islamic university system began to develop an ambitious civic education curriculum that was to fill the space left by changes to the ideological Pancasila courses that had been compulsory in the Suharto era. The program's goal was to equip students with the prerequisite understanding, knowledge, and skills in order to participate in the democratic political discourse and shape the country's democratic future. Consequently, it has emphasized participatory strategies for teaching and learning that will allow students to exercise the critical skills required in the practice of democracy next to the development of new curriculum materials.

The textbooks developed for the new civic education courses emphasize the compatibility of democratic and pluralist principles with fundamental Islamic values. In their analysis of the teaching materials, Jackson and Bahrissalim (2007) point to the combination of Islamic notions of citizenship and state with western traditions of democratic pluralism and civil society as a defining feature of the curriculum (p. 42). The discussion of different terms for civil society in the Indonesian debate is used as illustration. Among the terms available in the Indonesian discourse on civil society, the English "civil society" or its direct Indonesian translation, *masyarakat sipil*, is contrasted with the term *masyarakat madani*. The latter reflects an Islamic orientation that is captured in the use of the Arabic word *madani*. Although *madani* functions as the Arabic cognate for "civil," its connotations also directly connect it to central norms and values of Islam and the Muslim community that developed in the city of Medina at the time of Prophet Muhammad. The late Nurcholish Madjid, one of Indonesia's leading neo-modernist thinkers, in particular employed the term *masyarakat madani* to refer to the Constitution of Medina that regulated the rights and responsibilities of different religious groups in the early Muslim community. As an Islamic reference point for the conceptualization of civil society, *masyarakat madani* is not identical with western social-scientific concepts, but it is also not entirely different. Its use in the textbook materials, however, demonstrates the possibility to scale up normative Islamic principles of civic inclusion to promote respect for pluralism as well as religious and cultural rights of a diverse population.

The new civic education curriculum was piloted at the Syarif Hidayatullah State Islamic Institute in Jakarta in 2000. Following the successful pilot, the program was implemented across all campuses in the state Islamic system of higher education in the subsequent year. These accomplishments are especially noteworthy because of the central position the system occupies within the country's various Islamic educational networks. Numerous private Islamic colleges and universities have implemented their own versions of the state system's new civic education curriculum, most notably the institutions associated with the Muhammadiyah. The significance of these developments, as Azra *et al.* noted, is underscored by the fact that the state Islamic higher education system remains the preferred choice of post-secondary education for madrasa and pesantren graduates for whom it fulfills the role of a "cultural broker" between the different institutions and orientations in the national education system (Azra *et al.* 2007, p. 190). This role is further amplified by the fact that a growing number of madrasa and pesantren teachers receive their academic training in the state system (ibid.). These developments are likely to extend the influence of the civic culture promoted by the state Islamic universities to other institutions within the national education system, including the mostly privately organized pesantrens and madrasas.

The private educational networks of the Muhammadiyah and Nahdlatul Ulama

Most of Indonesia's private Islamic schools, both madrasas and pesantrens, are connected to one of Indonesia's leading Muslim mass organizations. The pesantrens are affiliated with the traditionalist Nahdlatul Ulama (NU) and its network of Islamic scholars or kiais, whereas the modernist Muhammadiyah primarily has championed the development of madrasa education. Despite the differences in their theological orientations, both organizations are united in their self-understanding as social welfare organizations with pronounced emphases on education. Both Muhammadiyah and NU have displayed openness to educational reform and cooperation with the state over the past decades. The state's attempts to integrate private schools more closely into the national education system intensified in the 1970s with the granting of degree equivalency to Islamic schools that adopted a standardized government curriculum of 30 percent religious and 70 percent general studies. A majority of Islamic schools, both madrasas and pesantrens, have since begun to teach the government-accredited curriculum and essentially have been transformed into general schools. In the transition to democracy after 1998, both NU and Muhammadiyah have continued to avoid direct involvement in party politics and instead affirmed their place in the sphere of civil society. Leading officials of both organizations have consistently spoken out against the establishment of an Islamic state or attempts to enshrine Islamic Law in the constitution and instead affirmed commitment to democratic reform, gender equality, human rights, and multi-religious citizenship (e.g., Mitsuo *et al.* 2001). Support for interfaith respect and inclusive forms of citizenship are reflected in initiatives and developments in the educational institutions of both organizations.

The Muhammadiyah has a history of educational innovation that includes a long tradition of successful educational reform dating back to the beginnings of the Muslim modernist movement in the early decades of the twentieth century. It has continued to upgrade its educational programs to respond to the growing demand for citizenship education in Indonesia's transition to democracy. The development of a new civic education program for its university system stands out among curricular initiatives aimed at promoting open and inclusive forms of citizenship.[3] The program was launched in 2003 after a critical assessment of the new civic education program in the state Islamic university system as well as older civic education programs within the Muhammadiyah system. Similar to the state system's program, instructional methodologies foster participatory learning and critical thinking aimed at democratizing the student's learning experience; course materials focus on issues such as democracy, civil society, human rights, and tolerance; and, much like in the state Islamic university program, Islamic concepts of citizenship and the state are brought into conversation with western theories and practices. Jackson and Bahrissalim, however, point out that the degree of this integration differs. True to the Muhammadiyah's reformist ideological orientation, Islamic concepts grounded in the Qur'an and the prophetic tradition or Sunna provide the primary reference point in the discussion (Jackson and Bahrissalim 2007, p. 50). The differences notwithstanding, the Muhammadiyah program displays an open and plural orientation in its approach to civic education by foregrounding the compatibility of core values in the Islamic tradition with democratic pluralism and civil society. Following the successful implementation of the civic education program in its university system, the Muhammadiyah has begun to put into practice a similar program in its network of secondary schools.

Creative efforts at generating trust across religious and communal boundaries and at promoting a public discourse marked by civility and respect for the rights of others are also evident in Indonesia's pesantren tradition. Similar to the Muhammadiyah schools, the past decades have seen the integration of many pesantrens into the national education system as a majority of them adopted government curricula or incorporated formal schools. Educational initiatives to support the democratization process have also gathered momentum within the pesantren tradition. These efforts are often carried out in cooperation with local or national non-governmental organizations (NGOs) such as the Indonesian Society for Pesantren and Community Development Perhimpunan Pengembangan Pesantren dan Masyarakat (P3M). The involvement of NGOs in the pesantren tradition has a history that began in the New Order period and was initially aimed at using the pesantrens as motors for community development, particularly in rural communities (Oepen and Karcher 1988). Since the late 1990s, another wave of NGOs has emerged that seek to advance a new discourse and practice in the pesantren tradition on significant societal issues from democracy to interfaith relations and gender equality. As van Bruinessen observed, "[m]ost of the Muslim NGOs that flourished since the 1990s have shown themselves very open-minded towards non-Muslims and eager to engage in inter-religious dialogue and joint activities" (Bruinessen 2003). The result of these developments has been an expansive network of scholars and activists affiliated with NU and the pesantren system who embrace religious diversity and the empowerment of civil society. A select number of pesantrens have even distinguished themselves nationally for their work in peacebuilding and the promotion of interfaith harmony.[4]

Politically radical and non-cooperative Islamic schools
The accommodating trends in Indonesia's Islamic schools described previously are not uncontested within the Islamic educational scene. Among the country's Islamic schools are found a small but highly visible number of institutions that propagate essentially non-cooperative political convictions and, in some cases, openly and violently challenge the ideals of Indonesian nationhood and the country's pluralist constitution in favor of the establishment of an Islamic state. A report by the ICG (2003) implicated several Islamic schools as centers of militant networks in Southeast Asia. Among these, Pesantren Ngruki in Central Java has received the most attention internationally. Its co-founder, Abu Bakar Ba'asyir, has been considered the spiritual leader of the Southeast Asian Jemaah Islamiyah (JI), a network believed to be responsible for some of the most atrocious terrorist attacks in Indonesia of the recent past. Although the extent of Ba'asyir's and the school's direct involvement in terrorist activities has been assessed differently by observers of the Indonesian scene, Ba'asyir is certainly among the harshest opponents of Indonesian nationalism and his public statements are unapologetically anti-democratic, anti-pluralist, anti-western, and anti-Jewish (Behrend 2003). These positions are reflected in some of the teaching materials at Ngruki in which nationalism is described as inimical to Islam and a form of polytheism, Islamic law put forth as the only appropriate basis for the state, and students are taught to avoid inter-religious relations (Hefner 2009, pp. 85–6).

Only a very small number of Islamic schools share Ngruki's political radicalism. Yet, the school is not unique in its broader social and political goals. Efforts at using the structures of their schools to bring about broader changes to Indonesian society and state have taken hold in a number of educational networks since the 1990s. Most recently, Hefner has analyzed these schools through the prism of social movement theory and pointed to the new quality of their educational mission that goes beyond the transmission of Islamic knowledge to individual students to include the use of schools and their educational programs to effect the Islamization of Indonesian society and, ultimately, the institutions of the state (Hefner 2009, pp. 70–91). They range from schools associated with moderate Islamist groups such as the Prosperous Justice Party (PKS) and the Hidayatullah organization to politically more radical schools akin to Ngruki, and finally include the puritanical and often politically passive Wahhabi–Salafi schools that are ideologically and financially connected to the Middle East (ibid.). Although these educational networks of some hundred schools are characterized by varying levels of acceptance of Indonesian nationalism and their participation in the political process, they are ideologically united in an outspoken anti-pluralist stance and anti-western bias. While it is not warranted to assume that such orientations will inevitably give rise to violence and militancy in these schools, it is clear that no positive value is assigned to religious or ideological diversity, and in most instances, socializing with non-Muslims or with Muslims who do not share the same ideological convictions is avoided on principle.

Islamic confessional education as model for peace education and tolerance

What is striking about the programs and approaches developed by Muslim educators in response to Indonesia's ongoing democratization is the diversity of ideological temperaments and political persuasions that they reveal. Far from monolithic, the country's Islamic education scene is characterized by an ongoing debate among Muslim educators over the political function of Islamic education. Without homogenizing this plurality, two general trends stand out. First, far from affirming the Orientalist stereotype of a static and unchanging Islamic tradition, Indonesian Islamic educational traditions have revealed themselves to be highly responsive to the changing socio-political and educational demands in their communities. Such openness is not an entirely new phenomenon either. Dating back to the early decades of the twentieth century, the successful educational reforms among Muslim modernists helped demonstrate to educators the compatibility of Islamic and general education and prepared the ground for future reform efforts. This responsiveness, second, is paralleled by the tendency among a majority of Muslim educators to accommodate Indonesian nationalism and the multi-religious and multi-ethnic foundations of the state. Although highly visible, only a small fraction of Islamic schools, on the fringes of a moderate educational mainstream, can be considered politically radical, and an even smaller minority has pursued broad political transformation in militant ways. The majority of Muslim schools are under the moderating influence of organizations such as the Muhammadiyah and NU that continue to have affirmed their dedication to public welfare and commitment to political reform.[5]

Perhaps even more surprising than the generally politically moderate outlook is that some of the country's most progressive educational programs addressing civic values of tolerance and co-citizenship are advanced by confessional-oriented Islamic schools. As has been noted earlier, what stands out about these initiatives is that they take place within settings that aim at nurturing commitment to the Islamic tradition and rarely, if at all, teach about other religions. By contrast, interfaith-oriented educational models are still the exception. Only a very small number of private religious schools have developed non-confessional or interfaith models of religious education, although these do not meet the terms of the 2003 Education Law (Leirvik 2004, p. 232). Given the limitations of the law and the new national curriculum noted previously, it may not be surprising that some Islamic institutions have developed their own materials and approaches outside of or in addition to the requirements of the national curriculum. This has been made possible in part by decentralization policies put in place after 1998 that have freed schools from the limiting control of the state and granted them greater educational autonomy. Decentralization alone, however, does not suffice to explain why Muslim educators have been willing and able to introduce progressive approaches to religious and civic education in their schools. In a comparative analysis of religious education models in Muslim-majority countries, Leirvik (2004) points to a number of additional triggers for the development of more inclusive designs. Next to the experience of political change and inter-communal conflict, he identifies the existence of international impulses as a further shaping influence on national educational programs (ibid., p. 230).

Internationally supported programs in the educational sector have a history in Indonesia that dates back into the New Order period. With the 1990s and increasingly after the events of September 11, 2001, international agencies such as The Asia Foundation, USAID, and the Ford Foundation have funded programs to improve the quality of education in Indonesian Islamic schools that emphasize in particular values of democracy and tolerance.[6] The high visibility of foreign sponsorship has featured prominently among the criticisms of the discourse on pluralism advanced in these educational initiatives. Anti-western bias is not the prerogative of non-cooperative or radicalized schools alone. Public discourse challenging pluralism as a western and thus alien concept to Islam has intensified following the 2005 fatwa by the Indonesian Council of Ulama (MUI) that declared pluralism, liberalism, and secularism to be western values and thus antithetical to traditions of Islamic thought (Gillespie 2007). In their analysis of the anti-pluralism discourse in Indonesia, Bagir and Cholil (2008) identify various recurring themes. Prominently among them are not only the criticisms of a "westernization" of Islam but also a theologically motivated objection that pluralism inevitably will lead to relativism and a weakening of commitment to Islam. While such opposition not necessarily entails, as Bagir and Cholil's analysis points out, a wholesale rejection of religious plurality as a social reality, the predominant mode of responding to such diversity, is non-engagement, or, simply letting the other be.

It is in response to these foundational questions of how to negotiate commitment to Islamic identity with openness to religious diversity that the educational programs discussed in this chapter make two significant contributions to the wider Indonesian discourse on co-citizenship and interfaith relations. Against the notion that the discourse on pluralism is merely derivative of western concepts, the ability of Muslim educators to develop normative Islamic frameworks that ascribe a positive value to religious diversity not only demonstrates that pluralist perspectives can be accommodated in Islam but that such positive value can be consistently derived from normative principles of the Islamic tradition. In other words, religious diversity is assigned a positive value not in spite of a principled commitment to the Islamic tradition but precisely because of it. A second and related point addresses the fear that any serious accommodation of other religious traditions must inevitably lead to a weakening of commitment to one's own religion. Rather than leading to a relativistic elimination of strong convictions, Islamic educational models that allow students to experience their tradition as a resource for tolerance can deepen students' confessional identities in the Islamic tradition rather than weakening them and will in turn contribute to the development of what Walzer (1994) calls "thick" motivations for tolerance that are grounded in and sustained by deep confessional convictions.

Finally, it will be prudent not to overestimate the role Islamic education can play in the promotion of interfaith harmony but to keep the contributions of educational institutions to tolerance and peace in perspective. Much will depend on the government's ability to curb religious intolerance through policy choices and committed efforts to uphold these by law enforcement. In conjunction with other institutions in Indonesian society, however, Islamic education can and often does provide models for the wider society of how to develop a praxis of tolerance by negotiating Islamic and national identities.

Works cited

Azra, Azyumardi, Dina Afrianty, and Robert W. Hefner, 2007, "Pesantren and Madrasa: Muslim Schools and National Ideals in Indonesia," in Robert W. Hefner, and Muhammad Q. Zaman, eds, *Schooling Islam: The Culture and Politics of Modern Muslim Education*, Princeton, NJ: Princeton University Press, pp. 172–97.

Bagir, Zainal Abidin, and Suhadi Cholil, 2008, *The State of Religious Pluralism in Indonesia: A Literature Review*, Yogakarta, Indonesia: Center for Religious & Cross-Cultural studies (Gadjah Mada Graduate School), accessed on April 9, 2011, http://www.hivos.net/content/download/2762/23740/file/PMS%201%202008%20Bagir%20and%20Cholil%20_brown_.pdf.

Baidhawy, Zakiyuddin, 2007, "Building Harmony and Peace through Multiculturalist Theology-Based Religious Education: An Alternative for Contemporary Indonesia," *British Journal of Religious Education* 22(1), January, pp. 15–30.

Behrend, Tim, 2003, "Preaching Fundamentalism: The Public Teachings of Abu Bakar Ba'asyir," *Inside Indonesia* 74, April-June, pp. 9–10.

Boland, B. J., 1971, *The Struggle of Islam in Modern Indonesia*, Slightly Revised Reprint 1982, The Hague: Martinus Nijhoff.

Bruinessen, Martin van, 2003, "Post-Suharto Muslim Engagements with Civil Society and Democracy," paper presented at the Third International Conference and Workshop "Indonesia in Transition," August 24-28, 2003, Universitas Indonesia, Depok, accessed on April 17, 2011, http://www.hum.uu.nl/medewerkers/m.vanbruinessen/publications/Post_Suharto_Islam_and_civil_society.htm.

Departemen Pendidikan Nasional (Badan Penelitian dan Pengembangan Pusat Statistik Pendidikan), 2008, *Ikhtisar Data Pendidikan Nasional (Tahun 2007/2008)*, accessed on May 12, 2011, http://www.kemdiknas.go.id/media/211066/bukusakufinal_0708.pdf.

Dhofier, Zamakhsyari, 1999, *The Pesantren Tradition. The Role of the Kyai in the Maintenance of Traditional Islam in Java*, Tempe, AZ: Program for Southeast Asian Studies.

Esposito, John L., and Dalia Mogahed, 2007, *Who Speaks for Islam? What a Billion Muslims Really Think*, New York: Gallup Press.

Gillespie, Piers, 2007, "Current Issues in Indonesian Islam: Analysing the 2005 Council of Indonesian Ulama Fatwa No. 7 Opposing Pluralism, Liberalism and Secularism," *Journal of Islamic Studies* 18(2), pp. 202–40.

Hassan, Riaz, 2007, "On Being Religious: Patterns of Religious Commitment in Muslim Societies," *The Muslim World* 97(3), July, pp. 437–78.

Hefner, Robert W., 2009, "Islamic Schools, Social Movements, and Democracy in Indonesia," in Robert W. Hefner, ed., *Making Modern Muslims: The Politics of Muslim Education in Southeast Asia*, Honolulu: University of Hawaii Press, pp. 55–105.

International Crisis Group (ICG), 2010, "Indonesia: 'Christianisation' and Intolerance," ICG Asia Briefing Policy 114, Jakarta/Brussels (November 24, 2010), accessed on March 25, 2011, http://www.crisisgroup.org.

International Crisis Groups (ICG), 2003, "Jemaah Islamiyah in Southeast Asia: Damaged but Still Dangerous," ICG Asia Report 63, Jakarta/Brussels (August 26, 2003), accessed on February 2, 2008, http://www.crisisgroup.org.

Jackson, Elisabeth, and Bahrissalim, 2007, "Crafting a New Democracy: Civic Education in Indonesian Islamic Universities," *Asia Pacific Journal of Education* 27(1), March, pp. 41–54.

Kementerian Agama Republik Indonesia, 2008, Data Keagamaan Tahun 2008, accessed on March 25, 2011, http://www.kemenag.go.id/index.php?a=artikel&id2=data2008.

Leirvik, Oddbjørn, 2004, "Religious Education, Communal Identity and National Politics in the Muslim World," *British Journal of Religious Education* 26(3), September, pp. 223–36.

Mitsuo, Nakamura, Sharon Siddique, and Omar Farouk Bajunid, eds., 2001, *Islam and Civil Society in Southeast Asia*, Singapore: Institute of Southeast-Asian Studies.

Mujani, Saiful, 2007, *Muslim Demokrat: Islam, Budaya Demokrasi, dan Partisipasi Politik di Indonesia Pasca-Orde Baru*, Jakarta: Gramedia Pustaka Utama.

Oepen, Manfred, and Wolfgang Karcher (Eds). (1988). *The Impact of Pesantren in Education and Community Development in Indonesia*, Berlin: Technical University Berlin.

Pew Global Attitudes Project, 2011, *Arab Spring Fails to Improve U.S. Image*, Washington, DC: Pew Research Center (May 17, 2011), accessed on May 21, 2011, http://pewglobal.org/files/2011/05/Pew-Global-Attitudes-Arab-Spring-FINAL-May-17-2011.pdf.

Pohl, Florian, 2006, "Islamic Education and Civil Society: Reflections on the *Pesantren* Tradition in Contemporary Indonesia," *Comparative Education Review* 50(3), August, pp. 389–409.

Raihani, 2007, "Education Reforms in Indonesia in the Twenty-first Century," *International Education Journal* 8(1), 172–83.

Walzer, Michael, 1994, *Thick and Thin: Moral Argument at Home and Abroad*, Notre Dame, IN: University of Notre Dame Press.

Notes

1. Surveys presented in Esposito and Mogahed (2007) and Mujani (2007) reveal levels of support for democracy, including a nuanced understanding of civil rights such as freedom of association, freedom of press, and legal equality including equal rights for women, that are comparable to polling data on these items in European and North American countries.

2. Confessional instruction, typically for two hours per week, has been part of the state curriculum since the 1950s, initially with the option for parental objection, but it became a requirement for all students enrolled in the public system in the 1960s (Boland 1971, p. 111).

3. Beyond the programmatic developments on the national level, sensitivity to diversity and differences is replicated in local initiatives at Muhammadiyah institutions. A particularly visible example has been the work of the Center for Cultural Studies and Social Change at the Muhammadiyah University of Surakarta, which has developed a program entitled "Muslim Tolerance and Appreciation for Multiculturalism" geared toward the development of a multicultural theological paradigm for religious education in Muhammadiyah schools and mosques (Baidhawy 2007, p. 22).

4. For a particularly celebrated example of a pesantren that has achieved national recognition for its leadership in interfaith initiatives and conflict resolution, see the discussion of Pesantren Al-Muayyad Windan in Central Java (Pohl 2006).

5. The politically moderate outlook of the educational mainstream is confirmed by a 2006 survey of Muslim educators that asked about support for democracy and pluralism (Hefner 2009). The survey results showed that educators' views did not differ significantly from the high level of support found among the general public. Notes Hefner, "[t]he educators' support for democracy and civil rights should dispel any impression that the religious establishment as a whole is a reactionary drag on an otherwise pluralist public" (ibid., p. 92).

6. Frequently, these initiatives focus on civic education programs as in the case of The Asia Foundation that has been involved in the development of the civic education program in the state Islamic system of higher education. It subsequently also supported similar efforts in the Muhammadiyah universities. Other prominent international agencies with a history that includes sponsorship of NGO activism in the pesantren scene are The Ford Foundation and USAID.

CROSSCURRENTS

AN INTERVIEW WITH ARJIA RINPOCHE

Pamela D. Winfield

In 1952, at the age of two, Arjia Rinpoche was recognized as the eighth reincarnation of the head abbot of the culturally rich and historically powerful Kumbum Monastery in Amdo, Eastern Tibet (alt. Qinghai province, China). His training was cut short, however, in 1958 when the Great Leap Forward and subsequent Cultural Revolution ushered in an unprecedented period of persecution and destruction of Tibet's living and material Buddhist heritage. After sixteen years of forced manual labor, Arjia Rinpoche was allowed to receive Dharma instruction again and resumed his previously ordained role as Kumbum's head abbot. Assisted by the Panchen Lama (second only to the Dalai Lama in terms of institutional authority and the highest-ranking Buddhist leader still in Tibet at the time), Arjia Rinpoche successfully navigated the political minefield of the Chinese Buddhist bureaucracy to protect and advance Buddhism from within. His story and the story of the Politburo's sinister and cynical attempt to control Tibetan politics through its own puppet Panchen Lama "reincarnation" are chronicled in his autobiographical *Surviving the Dragon: A Tibetan Lama's Account of 40 Years Under Chinese Rule*. The following conversation informs and updates readers of the political situation in Tibet and further explains his political involvements and crisis of conscience that compelled him to flee Tibet in 1998. At the time, this made him the highest-ranking lama to leave since the Dalai Lama in 1959.

Editor's Note: Many thanks to Mary Pattison of the TMBCC for transcribing and formatting Rinpoche's responses.

Question: What are the major political challenges facing Buddhism in Tibet/China today?

Response

1. The Communists are not only non-religious, they are also afraid of religion. The main reason is that a religion gathers people together under its umbrella, and any group of people gathered together may be a threat against the regime. For example, the Falung Gong organization has been persecuted by the Chinese Government because it fears that its members are being obedient and are controlled by someone other than the government. The same is with Christianity and Tibetan Buddhism as the Government fears the power of the Pope and the Dalai Lama. The Government is not afraid of Taoism as it is a very Chinese religion. Taoists are of the Chinese culture and speak the Chinese language. The actual beliefs of a religion are not the reason for the fear; instead, it is the fear of losing power over the people.

2. The monasteries have lost their religious mission and have become tourist traps. In the 1950s, before the Cultural Revolution, the Communists tried to stomp out religion, but they couldn't succeed. They managed to stop overt religious practices, but the hearts of the people were not affected. In the 1980s, the "open policy" appeared to lessen control, but instead the control merely became more subtle. The Communists turned the monasteries into commercial ventures. The economy is the main thing. Kumbum Monastery in Amdo, Tibet, has 10,000 visitors each day, and the monks are constantly doing pujas for money and have become businessmen.

3. The Communists do not really follow their Constitution. The leaders follow their laws only if they find the laws useful. Most of the Chinese people today do not care about religion, and there is a general lack of morality in the populace. For example, human organs are sold for profit; prisoners are sometimes killed for their organs. Monks don't practice ethical behavior and care only about wealth, have wives, and have become the "protectors" of big businessmen.

Question: What solutions are Buddhists finding to these challenges?

Response

1. There are no black and white solutions. Everything is a grayish tinge. You may say that 50% of the people are bad and 50% are good. Of the "good 50%," 30% percent of these are very good. In some places, small monasteries focus intently on their spiritual practices. Even in some of the larger monasteries, you will find some earnest practitioners.
2. Some monasteries are involved in charity work. "Engaged Buddhism" is a new, but very good thing. For example, many monks have worked hard at relief work for those devastated by the recent earthquakes. This is very good and very positive.
3. In recent years, many Chinese have become Buddhists for many different reasons. Some of these people are real scholars who are searching for the "essence of Buddhism." Some Tibetan lamas go to the Chinese to give them teachings. Perhaps in the future, the situation will see great improvement. However, these "conversions" are only on an individual basis as groups fear the Chinese government.

Question: What is your own personal experience with Chinese political life?

Response

1. I was oppressed by the government during the Cultural Revolution and was forced to work in a labor camp for sixteen years.
2. After the 1980s, I was promoted to high positions and re-established as Abbot of Kumbum Monastery, but only so that the Chinese government could control Tibetan Buddhist leaders and thereby control the Tibetan people. We always had to work out compromises to create solutions and opportunities to protect and preserve the religion. This depended on the individual. If a lama was only thinking about his own comfort, then the results were terrible. Otherwise, he could do much good.
3. The appointment of a Panchen Lama by the Chinese government was an event that clearly shows how the Communists try to manipulate the Buddhist religion for their own benefit. Let me explain this situation.
   - Briefly, it is a Tibetan tradition that when lama from a monastery passes away, his rebirth is sought for and when the child is found, he

is taken to that monastery and reared by the monks in the traditions of the Buddhist religion and in the specific religious practices of that monastery.
- The two highest lamas in Tibet are the Dalai Lama and the Panchen Lama—they are likened to the "sun and the moon." It is traditional that when the Dalai Lama passes away, the monastery of the Panchen Lama finds his reincarnation, and when the Panchen Lama passes away, the monastery of the Dalai Lama finds his reincarnation.
- In 1959, the Dalai Lama had to leave Tibet because of the invasion of the Chinese Communists. The 10th Panchen Lama remained in Tibet and worked hard to help the Tibetan people who were suffering under the oppression of the Communists. During the Cultural Revolution, he was imprisoned for thirteen years. When he was freed, he continued to work for the benefit of the Tibetan people. Unfortunately, he died suddenly in 1989.
- At that time, the Dalai Lama was living in exile in Dharamsala, India, but immediately he began to consider the finding of the reincarnation of the Panchen Lama—following Tibetan tradition. At first, the Chinese government was willing to tolerate his involvement in this endeavor, but after the events of Tiananmen Square, they withdrew their cooperation and even imprisoned Chadrel Rinpoche, Abbot of Tashi Lhumpo Monastery, a lama that was working under the direction of the Dalai Lama, along with others, to find the Panchen Lama's incarnation.
- In 1995, the Dalai Lama recognized a five-year-old Tibetan child, Gedhun Choekyi Nyima, as the reincarnation of the Panchen Lama. Immediately, the Chinese government objected and abducted the child. He has not been heard of since that time.
- The Chinese then selected their own Panchen Lama by holding a Golden Urn Ceremony, which they claimed was both their right and was also a long-held tradition of the Tibetan people. There is some evidence that a Golden Urn ceremony was conducted during the Qing dynasty to recognize both the Dalai Lama and the Panchen Lama; however, this ceremony was never acknowledged by the Tibetan people.
- The Golden Urn ceremony, held in Lhasa, was actually "rigged" as the Chinese Communists had already decided on their choice. Gyalcain Norbu, selected by the People's Republic of China, was formally

installed on November 11, 1995, as the 11th Panchen Lama. We Tibetan lamas were required to prostrate before him, even though we knew in our hearts that he was not the true 11th Panchen Lama.

- The Chinese Communists' control of the 11th Panchen Lama is an attempt to ensure that when the present Dalai Lama passes away, they will have control over his reincarnation. However, the present Dalai Lama insists today that politically speaking, the control of the Tibetan Government-in-Exile is in the hands of a democratically elected prime minister and Kashag (Tibetan Cabinet). Spiritually speaking, the Dalai Lama says that his rebirth will not be born in Tibet.
- The Chinese Communists continue to interfere with Tibetan Buddhist traditions by saying that all tulkus (reincarnated lamas) must be certified by the government before they can be recognized.

4. I was told that I would have to become the tutor of the Chinese-chosen 11th Panchen Lama. My uncle, Gyayak Rinpoche, had been the 10th Panchen Lama's spiritual teacher and I was to follow his footsteps. Rather than compromise my loyalty to the Tibetan people and His Holiness the Dalai Lama, in 1998, I decided to flee from Tibet and live with a clear conscience but far away from my native land.

Postscript: In 2005, the Dalai Lama appointed Arjia Rinpoche to direct the Tibetan-Mongolian Buddhist Cultural Center in Bloomington, IL, after his own brother and former director fell ill.

CROSSCURRENTS
CONTRIBUTORS

Jennifer Eichman currently teaches at Moravian College, PA. Her work, spanning the sixteenth through twenty-first centuries, examines Chinese Buddhist culture from the perspective of social history and material culture. In 2010, she was awarded a Chung-hua Institutes Book-writing Grant for her forthcoming work on the *Spiritual Peregrinations of a Chinese Buddhist Network*.

Amanda J. Huffer (Ph.D. University of Chicago, 2010). Her dissertation entitled, "Darshan in a Hotel Ballroom: Amritanandamayi Ma's (Amma's) Communities of Devotees in the United States" is an ethnographic study of a transnational guru movement focused on the historical context of the development of Hinduism in the United States. Her research specialties are South Asian Religions, American Religions, New Religious Movements, Gender Studies, Immigration, and Ethnographic Methodology. Her recently published works include "Female Immigration as a Catalyst for Ritual Practice: A Social History of Hinduism in the United States" (*Journal of Hindu Studies*, 2010) and a translation of the Sadvi Shakti Parishad's "Mātṛmahāśakti: A Commemorative Volume" (2007). She is currently working on her book manuscript entitled, *Hugs and Kisses: Feminizing the Face of Global Hinduism*. Prior to her recent appointment at University of California, Riverside, she served as visiting faculty at Austin College.

Laurel Kendall (Ph.D. Columbia 1979 with distinction) is chair of the Anthropology Division at the American Museum of Natural History where she is also curator of Asian Ethnographic Collections. Her long acquaintance with Korea began as a U.S. Peace Corps Volunteer in the early 1970s. Kendall is the author of several volumes on the subject of Korea, shamans, modernity, gender, and popular religion, including *Shamans, Housewives, and Other Restless Spirits: Women in Korean Ritual Life* (Hawaii, 1985), *The Life and Hard Times of a Korean Shaman: of Tales and the Telling of Tales* (Hawaii, 1988), *Getting Married in Korea: of Gender, Morality, and Modernity* (California, 1996) as well as many articles and edited and coedited volumes. Her most recent book, *Shamans, Nostalgias, and the IMF: South Korean Popular Religion in Motion*, won the Yim Suk-jay prize as the best work of anthropology about Korea by a non-Korean scholar through 2009. Kendall has also engaged in collaborative research with colleagues in Vietnam, including the exhibit "Vietnam: Journeys of Body, Mind, and Spirit" (opened 2003), which won her a Friendship Medal from the Government of Vietnam.

Mark Patrick McGuire is a professor of Humanities and cofounder of a campus sustainability initiative at John Abbott College in Montréal. A documentary filmmaker and activist, his work has been screened at festivals and conferences in Australia, Europe, North America, East and South Asia. His next film is a meditation on the impacts of war on soldiers and their families.

Levi McLaughlin is assistant professor of Religion at Wofford College in South Carolina. He received his B.A. and M.A. in East Asian Studies from the University of Toronto and his Ph.D. in Religion from Princeton University. Levi specializes in the study of religion and society in modern and contemporary Japan.

Florian Pohl (Ph.D. Temple University) is assistant professor in religious studies at Emory University's Oxford College in Oxford, Georgia. His field of research is Southeast Asian Islam with a special focus on questions of contemporary religious expression and public life. Among his recent publications are "Interreligious Harmony and Peacebuilding in Indonesian Islamic Education," in *Peace Psychology in Asia* ed. Christina Montiel and Noraini Noor (New York: Springer, 2009), 147–160 and *Islamic Education and the Public Sphere: Today's Pesantren in Indonesia* (Muenster/New York: Waxmann, 2009). For the past five years, he also has been affiliated through research and teaching with the Center for Religious and Cross-cultural Studies (CRCS) at Gadjah Mada University in Yogyakarta, Indonesia.

Pamela D. Winfield (Ph.D. Temple University) is assistant professor in the Department of Religious Studies and coordinator of Asian Studies at Elon University, Elon, NC. She specializes in Japanese Buddhist art and doctrine. She is currently cochair of the Religions of Asia Section of the American Academy of Religion (AAR/Southeastern Region) and the Southeastern Commission for the Study of Religion (SECSOR). As a former Coolidge Fellow, she also serves on the editorial board of *CrossCurrents* and on the Board of Directors of the Association of Religion and Intellectual Life (ARIL).

www.ingramcontent.com/pod-product-compliance
Lightning Source LLC
Chambersburg PA
CBHW040259170426
43193CB00020B/2951